From Your Friends At **The MAILBOX**®

Holidays
Through The Year

PROJECT EDITORS:
Ada Goren
Jan Trautman

EDITORS:
Michele Dare, Jayne Gammons, Mackie Rhodes, Allison Ward

ARTISTS:
Cathy Spangler Bruce, Pam Crane, Nick Greenwood,
Clevell Harris, Susan Hodnett, Sheila Krill,
Theresa Lewis, Rob Mayworth, Kimberly Richard,
Rebecca Saunders, Donna K. Teal

COVER ARTISTS:
Nick Greenwood, Kimberly Richard

www.themailbox.com

Manufactured in the United States
10 9 8 7 6 5 4 3 2 1

Table Of

Contents

HELLO, NEW YEAR!

Greet the new year with these festive activities filled with fashion, fun, and fizz.

ideas contributed by Kimberli Carrier

NEW YEAR CROWNS

Youngsters will welcome the new year in regal style when they make these creative crowns. To make one, cut a zigzag edge along one long side of a 3" x 9" construction-paper strip. Glue the die-cut numerals for the new year onto the paper strip; then glue glitter onto the numerals. After the glue dries, attach the numeral strip to a sentence strip as shown. Write the message "Happy New Year!" on the strip and embellish it with glitter pens, stickers, and other festive craft items. Fit each child's crown to her head and staple the ends. Then encourage youngsters to wear their crowns throughout the day as they offer New Year's greetings to one another.

RING IN THE NEW YEAR

Add some sparkle to the new year with these decorative bells. To prepare, cover your art table with newspaper. Then provide a small Styrofoam® cup, a sparkly pipe-cleaner half, and a jingle bell for each child. Have each child paint his cup with diluted glue. Than have him sprinkle glitter evenly over the cup and set it aside to dry. Use a blunt pencil to poke two holes in the cup bottom. Have the child thread the pipe-cleaner half through the loop in the jingle bell. Then slip the jingle bell into the cup and pull the two pipe-cleaner ends through the holes. Twist the pipe-cleaner ends together to create a handle for the bell. Invite youngsters to ring along to this rhyme as they welcome the new year.

Ring-a-ling-a, ding-a-ling!
A new year has begun.
[2000] will be a year
Just full of learning fun!

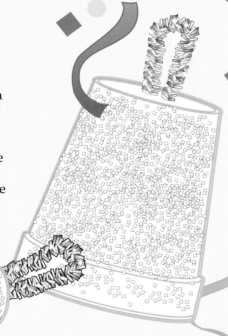

A NEW YEAR'S BLAST

Celebrate the arrival of the new year with this colorful chant. To prepare for this activity, place a class supply of party horns in assorted solid colors in a bag. During a group time, pass the bag to each child. Have each child close his eyes as he removes a horn from the bag. Write his name on the horn with a permanent marker. Then ask the child to recite the chant below, filling in the blanks with his horn's color and the year. At the end of the chant, encourage him to give a spirited blast on his horn.

After each child has had a turn, further challenge youngsters' listening and color-recognition skills. Recite the chant several times, naming a different color each time you repeat it. Invite only the children with the named color to blow their horns each time. Youngsters are sure to have a blast with this activity!

[Color] horn, [color] horn, give a blast.
[Year] is here at last!

FIRST-DAY FIZZ

Bring in the new year with this bubbly treat!

FIRST-DAY FIZZ

(serves 1)

1 cup lemon-lime soda
1 scoop rainbow sherbet
1 tablespoon whipped topping
1 teaspoon sprinkles

Pour the soda into a clear plastic cup. Add the sherbet. Be sure to look and listen for the fizz! Top with whipped topping and sprinkles. Enjoy!

IN WITH THE NEW

"Out with the old. In with the new." Here's an idea to help youngsters grasp the meaning of this traditional saying—and to freshen up your classroom for the new year! In advance, prepare a goodie bag for each child by placing new school supplies—such as crayons, glue sticks, or pencils—into a small decorative gift bag. Add a new cubby label and/or desktag, too. As part of your New Year's celebration, ask youngsters to help you give your classroom a good cleaning. Have them clean out cubbies or desks and straighten up all your centers. When the classroom has that brand-new feel to it, present each child with a gift bag of new school goodies.

A WHOLE NEW YEAR

It's the beginning of an exciting new year—the perfect time to review the calendar and to preview special events for the upcoming year. To begin, bring in a calendar for the new year. Remind youngsters that a year has 12 months. Then flip each page of the calendar as the class names each month in sequence. Then go back to January and discuss any special dates or upcoming events that will take place this month. Repeat the process for each month. Finally, flip the calendar pages once again, this time inviting students to name their birthdays and point to them on the calendar as you go through the months. Wow! This whole new year is going to be a whole lot of fun!

ROOTIN'-TOOTIN' RESOLUTIONS

Now that students know what a resolution is, invite them to fine-tune their personal resolutions with these special horns. To prepare, duplicate a class supply of the resolution pattern (page 7) on white construction paper; then make several tagboard tracers of the horn pattern. Working with one small group at a time, have each child cut out his resolution pattern. Ask him to write/dictate a resolution for the new year on his cutout and then decorate the paper with colorful confetti. Next, have him trace the horn pattern onto the back of a piece of foil gift wrap. Instruct the child to cut out his horn and then label it with his name. Have him glue his resolution to the large end of the horn. Display the horns with a copy of the song "Resolution." Add some curling ribbon and confetti to the bulletin-board background to complete this festive display.

RESOLUTION SING-ALONG

After previewing the new year, introduce youngsters to a new word: *resolution*. Ask students to tell what they think this word might mean. Then explain that a resolution is a decision or promise to do a specific thing, such as cleaning one's room or being a good friend to others. Tell youngsters that many people make resolutions at the beginning of a new year. Then teach your class this song. If desired, invite students to ring their bells from "Ring In The New Year" (page 4) as they sing.

RESOLUTION

(sung to the tune of "Row, Row, Row Your Boat")

Res-res-resolution—
A promise I make to me.
As the new year rolls along
I'll try my best, you'll see!

Res-res-resolution—
A promise I make to me.
As the new year rolls along
I'll try my best, you'll see!

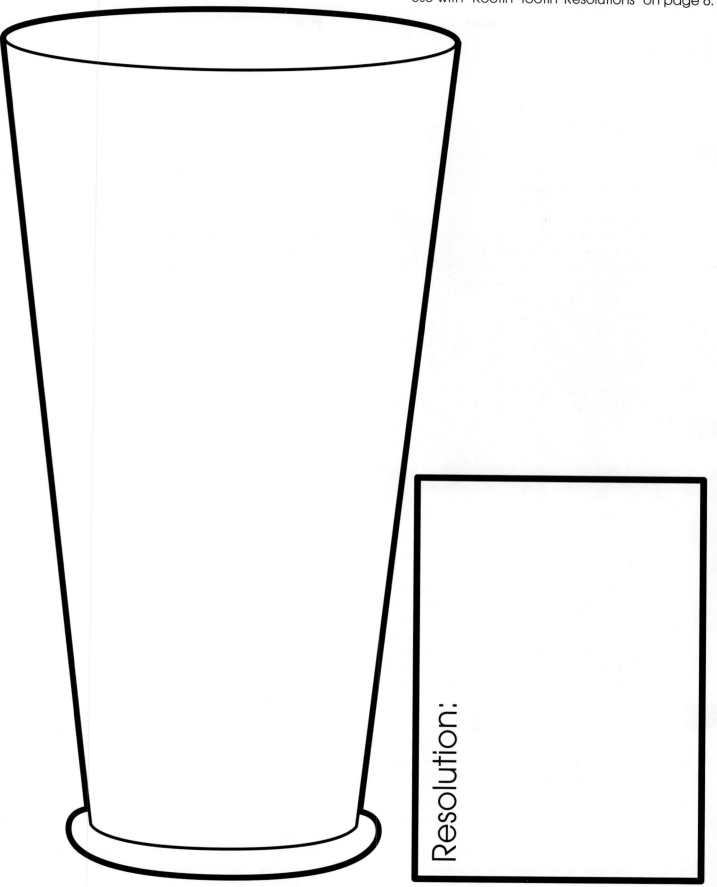

Resolution:

Martin Luther King Day

Martin Luther King, Jr., was a famous Black American who dreamed that one day all people would live in harmony. He worked very hard to spread peace, love, and understanding. Although Dr. King is no longer with us, his legacy of justice and friendship among people of different races lives on. His birthday is celebrated as a national holiday on the third Monday of January. Introduce Dr. King's dream of peace and understanding by celebrating his birthday with this collection of activities.

ideas contributed by Lynn Creede

Our Dreams

This cooperative book is a picture-perfect way to kick off a birthday celebration in honor of Dr. King! Read aloud Jean Marzollo's age-appropriate book *Happy Birthday, Martin Luther King* (Scholastic Inc.). Afterward, discuss Dr. King's famous dream, and explain that his *dream* was a hope or a wish for the future. Then invite youngsters to share their own dreams of peace and understanding. Provide each child with a sheet of white construction paper and ask her to illustrate her dream. Then have her dictate her dream as you write. Bind the students' completed pages between construction-paper covers. Title the book and place it in your classroom library for plenty of dreamy reading!

P-E-A-C-E

Sing this jolly tune to reinforce Dr. King's hopes for peace. For added learning fun, write the word *peace* on a chart and point to each letter as it is sung.

(sung to the tune of "Bingo")
There was a man who worked for peace.
His name was Dr. King.
P-E-A-C-E, P-E-A-C-E, P-E-A-C-E
Peace and understanding!

My dream is for everyone to have bunches of friends.

"Dove-ly" Prints

Create a peaceful display in honor of Dr. King's dream with this touching project. Explain to youngsters that white doves are worldwide symbols of peace; then invite each student to try her hand at this project. To make a dove print, paint your palm with white, washable tempera paint. Keeping your fingers together, press your hand onto dark blue construction paper. Repeat to make a desired number of prints. When the paint is dry, use tempera paint and a cotton swab (or small brush) to add a beak and an eye to each dove. Display the completed doves with the title "We Believe In Peace." How lovely!

Peace Puppets

These inviting dove puppets provide a fun way to reinforce students' understanding of Dr. King's desire for peace. To make one puppet, cut a six-inch white paper plate in half. Set one piece aside for the body, and then cut the other piece in half to form wings. Cut out a white construction-paper head and a yellow construction-paper beak. Glue the parts together as shown, adding a wiggle eye to the head. Complete the puppet by taping (or gluing) a tongue depressor to the back of the body. Place the puppets in your language center or dramatic-play area. Then encourage students to use the puppets to role-play teaching peace and spreading Dr. King's dream.

A Very Special Necklace

These charming necklaces will remind each student that peace begins with him. In advance, duplicate page 11 onto white construction paper for each child. To make one necklace, cut out the charm on the bold line. Turn your charm so that the words face you, and then write your name on the line and color the border. Turn the charm so the words face away from you, and then use markers to draw your face on the blank side. Glue on yarn hair. Next fold the charm over a 30-inch length of yarn and glue it shut. When the glue is dry, tie the necklace to fit. Invite each youngster to wear his special necklace whenever he shows peaceful behavior, such as helping a friend or talking to solve a problem. Dr. King would be proud!

Spread The Word

Dr. King's legacy lives on as people of all races continue to spread peace, love, and friendship. Have your little ones campaign to spread his message of hope throughout your school by inviting school personnel and other students to pledge peace. Provide each child with a sheet of construction paper and markers. Then have her draw a picture of a peace dove or an event in Dr. King's life. Have her dictate a brief invitation to pledge peace as you write it on her paper. Also leave a blank for a name and the date.

Display the pledges in your hallway with a title such as "We Say Yes To Peace!" Invite students and school personnel to walk by and sign up to pledge peace. Bet your campaign will attract lots of lasting peace pledges!

We Say Yes To Peace!

All Together Now!

Culminate your celebration of Dr. King's birthday with a peace parade through your school! Invite each child to don his necklace and carry his dove puppet (directions to make both are on page 9). For an extra-festive touch, give student volunteers bells to ring as they march. As you lead the parade around the school, play Red Grammer's *Teaching Peace* (Red Note Records) for additional musical accompaniment. This parade is sure to be a hit with students and a memorable tribute to Dr. King's dream.

More Martin Luther King, Jr., Literature

There are many books about Dr. King, but very few are appropriate for young children. You may need to paraphrase these selections for your little ones, but sharing these books will help them understand more about Dr. King's life and what he believed.

A Picture Book Of Martin Luther King, Jr.
Written by David A. Adler
Published by Holiday House, Inc.

Happy Birthday, Martin Luther King
Written by Jean Marzallo
Published by Scholastic Inc.

Young Martin Luther King, Jr.: "I Have A Dream"
Written by Joanne Mattern
Published by Troll Associates, Inc.

Martin Luther King Day
Written by Linda Lowery
Published by Carolrhoda Books, Inc.

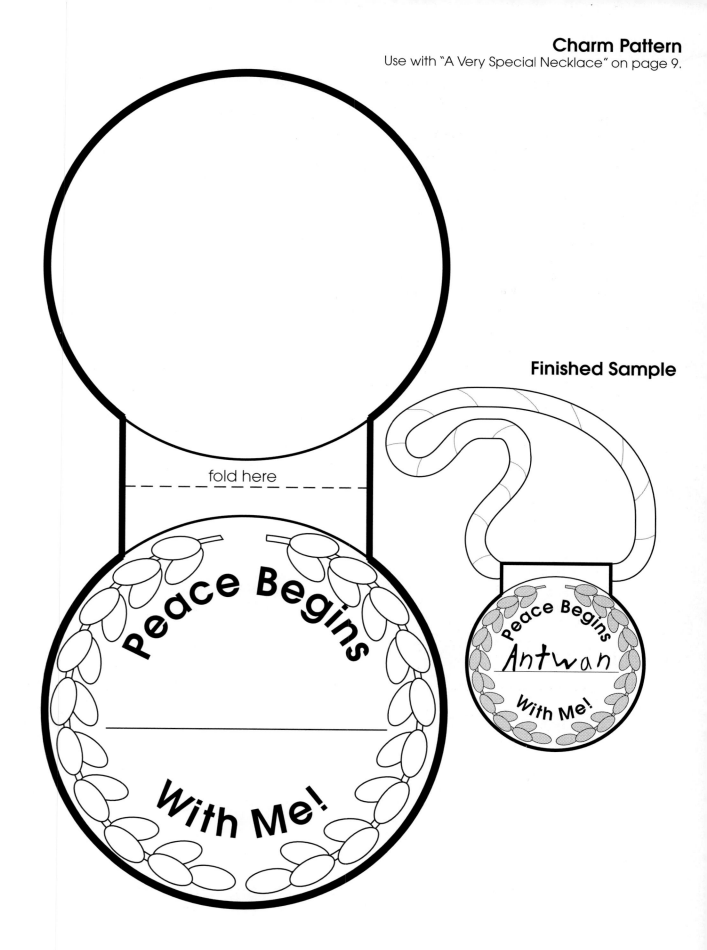

fold here

Finished Sample

Peace Begins With Me!

Peace Begins Antwan With Me!

Groundhogs Galore

Stir up youngsters' curiosity over these curious creatures with this collection of curriculum-related ideas.

by Mackie Rhodes

Groundhog Grab Bag

Youngsters will dig learning interesting information about groundhogs. Check out the list of groundhog facts below; then gather the articles that represent each piece of information and place them in a large bag. Invite student volunteers to remove the items one by one; then explain how each item relates to a groundhog. After they burrow through this bag of information, your groundhog gurus will eagerly scurry off to share their knowledge with family and friends.

A Groundhog…

- has a brown, furry coat (*a piece of brown craft fur*)
- has sharp teeth and claws (*a set of plastic teeth*)
- is about the size of a ten-pound bag of potatoes (*a potato*)
- eats plants, such as vegetables (*plastic vegetables*)
- digs an underground burrow or den (*a sand shovel*)
- sleeps, or *hibernates*, during the winter (*a small pillow*)
- whistles to warn other groundhogs of danger (*a whistle*)
- is considered by legend to be a weather predictor (*a die-cut sun shape*)

Shadow Watching

This calendar activity will keep youngsters interested in the weather throughout February. To prepare, make a tagboard copy of the groundhog pattern (page 15), adjusting the size to fit your class calendar squares. Trace the groundhog onto black construction paper and cut out a month's supply. Each school day, send a volunteer outdoors to check the weather and to look for his shadow. Back in the classroom, have him report the weather, and then attach a groundhog cutout to the calendar if he saw his shadow. At the end of the month, count and compare the number of days with and without groundhog shadows. After all this shadow watching, can students tell what type of weather enables a groundhog to see its shadow?

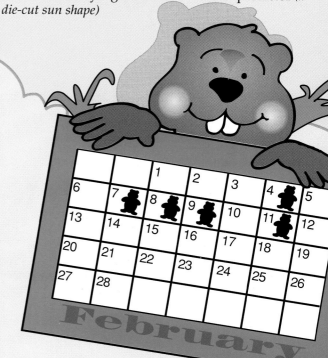

Shadow-Seeking Spud Bud

You may not have a real groundhog on Groundhog Day, but you and your students can make this cute substitute! Just use the potato you brought in for "Groundhog Grab Bag" (page 12) and a clear, contoured 20-ounce plastic soda bottle. Cut off the bottom of the bottle; then line it with brown tissue paper. Stand the dry potato upright in the bottle bottom, tucking more paper around the potato to achieve a snug fit. Poke two flat toothpicks into the top of the potato; then glue a construction-paper ear onto each one. Use craft glue to attach pom-pom paws, a tail, and a nose. Draw eyes and a mouth on the potato groundhog with a permanent marker. Post your groundhog outside your classroom on Groundhog Day; then invite youngsters to check for its shadow several times during the day. Will spring come early? Or will it be late?

carrot coins	spinach leaves	tomato chunks
卌 ‖	‖‖	‖

Groundhog Grub

Here's a tasty way to entice your growing groundhogs to nibble a nutritious vegetable snack. To begin, have each child create a simple groundhog headband. Prior to snacktime, have students help prepare a dish for each fresh vegetable to be served, such as carrot coins, tomato chunks, and spinach leaves. If desired, display the dishes with the groundhog created in "Shadow-Seeking Spud Bud." At snacktime, invite each child to don his headband and sample each vegetable. After he tastes the veggies, have him record a tally mark on a graph for each one that he likes. Count and compare the results with students. Which groundhog grub is the class favorite?

Groundhog Roundup

Invite youngsters to wear the groundhog headbands from "Groundhog Grub" for this action-packed color-matching game. To prepare, duplicate a class supply plus a few extra of the groundhog patterns (page 15) onto several construction-paper colors; then cut out each pattern. Place a few plastic hoops on the ground outdoors to represent groundhog burrows. Tape a different-colored groundhog cutout to each hoop. Then give each child a groundhog cutout to hold.

Begin by having one child with each color of groundhog stand in his corresponding burrow. The other groundhogs scatter in the area around the burrows. Blow a whistle (the groundhog's signal for danger) and have the scattered groundhogs begin to run around. Encourage each groundhog in a burrow to hurry to find a groundhog of the same color to bring back to the safety of his burrow. On the next whistle, the new groundhog in the burrow must find a color match in the same fashion. Play continues until all the same-color groundhogs are rounded up into the corresponding burrow.

Burrow Buddies

It's "a-maze-ing" how much fun youngsters will have with this relay game! Arrange two identical obstacle courses—or groundhog burrows—with items such as playground cones, box tunnels, and plastic hoops. Have students put on their groundhog headbands (see "Groundhog Grub" on page 13); then divide your class into two teams. Position half of each team at one end of its burrow, and the other half at the other end. Explain that, on a signal, a groundhog from each team will burrow through the course and then tag a teammate on the opposite end. The tagged burrow buddy will then negotiate the course in the opposite direction to tag a buddy on the other end. The game continues in this fashion until each groundhog has burrowed through the course. After completing the course, invite each team to perform this cheer:

Two, four, six, eight.
We're burrow buddies, and we're great!

Run across the room on all fours.

Groundhog Memory

Youngsters will develop some "hole-some" memory skills when they play this card game. To prepare the cards, cut out a quantity of black construction-paper circles to represent holes. Reduce one of the groundhog patterns (page 15) to fit onto a hole cutout. Then duplicate enough groundhogs for half of the holes. Also duplicate a supply of sentence boxes (page 15) for half of the holes. Glue each groundhog cutout and each sentence box onto a different hole. If desired, laminate the cards for durability.

Invite a small group of students to join you for a game. First spread the cards facedown on a table. Explain that a groundhog card and a sentence card make a match. Then instruct students to play the game like Memory®. Each time a player finds a match, invite her to perform the action described in the sentence.

Groundhog Patterns

Use with "Shadow Watching" on page 12, "Groundhog Roundup" on page 13, and "Groundhog Memory" on page 14.

Give a little whistle.

Jump three times.

Crawl around a chair.

Pretend to dig a burrow.

Stand tall and count to ten.

Crawl under a table.

Run across the room on all fours.

Scratch the ground five times.

Make up a silly ground-hog dance.

Run in a circle.

100 Hoorays For 100 Days!

Count on these lively ideas for celebrating the
100th day of school to fight off those midwinter blahs!

ideas contributed by Joe Appleton

Today Your Class...Tomorrow The World!

Just how big should your 100th day celebration be? Well, you could celebrate it as a class, as a grade level, as a school, or even as a school system! Depending on how big you decide to make your celebration, consider inviting a local newspaper or television station to photograph or film some of your festivities. Really make the 100th day of school a memorable one!

100 Hoorays For 100 Days!

A Banner Day

What better way to celebrate a banner day than with a banner? Invite students to help you create this decorative banner; then display it outside your classroom. Begin by cutting a 100-inch length of brightly colored bulletin-board paper (that's just over eight feet long). Write "100 Hoorays For 100 Days!" in large letters across the banner. Then have students help you decorate the remaining space with a chosen motif. Try one of the following or come up with your own 100-related design.
- 100 seasonal drawings or cutouts (such as snowflakes or hearts)
- 100 paint handprints
- 100 magazine pictures of animals
- 100 three-letter words

If your 100th day falls in February (National Children's Dental Health Month), you might even draw a *giant* mouth with 100 teeth! Smile!

100 Of This And 100 Of That...

Read aloud *Miss Bindergarten Celebrates The 100th Day Of Kindergarten* by Joseph Slate (Dutton Books). Then invite your students to bring in their own "wonderful, one-hundred-full" collections, just as Miss Bindergarten's students do in the story. Award a ribbon to each collector, in categories such as "most original collection," "smallest collection," "funniest collection," etc. Or make this a competition between classes. Choose a number of categories equal to the number of classes participating; then have a panel of judges (teachers) award prizes. How about 100 Hershey's® Kisses® or 100 extra minutes on the playground?

A 100-Hunting Hike

This small-group activity will have your youngsters hiking around your school to hunt for 100 items. Beforehand, discuss items that might be found in the quantity of 100, such as desks, tables, windows, steps, or doorknobs. Have the children in each small group choose one of the named items and estimate whether they will find fewer than 100, exactly 100, or more than 100 of their item. Then assign an adult helper to each group (or take the groups out one at a time). Give one child in each group a sheet of paper and a pencil to take on the hike. As you travel, have him use tally marks to record the group's findings.

When you return to the classroom, help each group total its tally marks. Divide a sheet of chart paper into three columns. Label one column "Fewer Than 100," one column "Exactly 100," and one column "More Than 100." Have each group tell you where to record its item on the chart. Were there exactly 100 of anything? Happy hunting!

Fewer than 100	Exactly 100	More than 100
73 tables		242 chairs
44 windows		
27 steps		

Rap-Rap-Rappin' On The 100th Day

Raise your hand if you like to rap! After teaching youngsters this easy rhyme and the accompanying hand motions, choose ten students to act it out. Of course, you won't be able to wrap up this activity until everyone has had a chance to get in on the act!

100th Day Rap

Gimme ten, gimme twenty,
Gimme thirty or more.

Three children jump up (one at a time) and hold up two hands.

Gimme forty, gimme fifty,
Gimme sixty on the floor.

Three more children up. All (including audience) slap hands on floor.

Gimme seventy, eighty, ninety,
Rap-rap-rappin' on the door.

Three more children up. All make fists and rap on imaginary doors.

Gimme one hundred fingers,
And a great big ROAR!

One more child up. Everyone roars.

And Now For Something A Little Quieter...

Use the "100th Day Rap" to reinforce numeral-recognition skills. Write the rhyme on sentence strips. Cut smaller strips sized to cover each number word. Program the smaller strips with the numerals 20, 30, 40, etc. Laminate all the strips for durability.

Display the rhyme in a pocket chart. Distribute the numeral cards to ten students. Repeat the rhyme slowly, asking the students to cover the number words with the matching numerals.

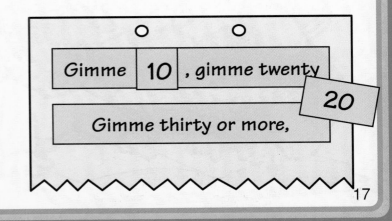

Gimme | 10 | , gimme twenty

20

Gimme thirty or more,

Food, Glorious Food!

This community-conscious activity will teach students about both math *and* sharing. Explain to your youngsters that while people often gather food and supplies for the poor and homeless during the holiday season, the need for food contributions remains great throughout the year. Since the 100th day of school usually falls in the postholiday, cold-weather months of January or February, it's an ideal time to sponsor a food drive. Challenge your students to collect 100 cans or boxes of food; then graph the results. Here's how to get started:

- Contact your local Food Bank, Salvation Army, or other appropriate nonprofit organization to discuss the details of food collection. (Contact Second Harvest National Network of Food Banks at 1-800-771-2303 to help locate food collection agencies near you.)
- Decide whether your food drive will be a class, grade-level, or schoolwide effort.
- Duplicate the note on page 19 and send a copy home with each child on the 90th day of school.
- Enlarge the can patterns on page 19. Then make a large supply of the enlarged patterns and cut them apart.

As each child brings in a food item, give her a can pattern. Ask her to color it, write her name on the back, and return it to you. Save these during the collection period. On the 100th day of school, prepare a giant wall graph. If you have more than one class or grade participating, make a heading for each group. Gather all the participants near the graph and invite each child to attach her pattern(s). Count and compare the number of food items donated by each group. Finish up with a rendition of the "100th Day Rap" on page 17.

Kindergarten 100th Day Food Collection

Mrs. Adams's Class	Mr. Jenkins's Class	Miss Ward's Class	Mrs. Taylor's Class	Mr. Andrews's Class

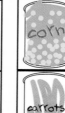

There's Got To Be A Morning After

After all the excitement, what do you do on the 101st day of school? Share *Walt Disney's One Hundred One Dalmatians: A Counting Book* by Fran Manushkin (Disney Press). The large format of this book makes it possible for students to join in as you count up all the dalmatians. Can they find all 101?

Dear Family:

We've almost reached the **100th day of school!** In honor of this special day, we are planning a unique celebration. In cooperation with _____, we are sponsoring a food collection drive. Our goal is to collect **100 cans and boxes of nonperishable food** by the 100th day of school.

This will be an excellent opportunity to practice our math skills! Each time your child brings a can or box of food to school for the drive, he or she will receive a paper can or box shape to color and personalize. On the 100th day of school, we'll be making a giant wall graph to show the results of our drive.

Please help us in our endeavor (and help the less fortunate in our community) by sending in one or more cans or boxes of nonperishable food by

_____.

(date)

Thanks so much for your support!

_____
(teacher's signature)

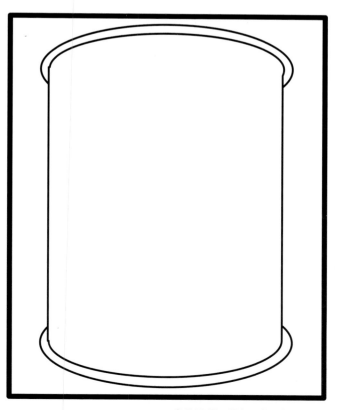

It's Presidents' Day!

Celebrate the birthdays of George Washington and Abraham Lincoln with these star-spangled ideas.

ideas contributed by Suzanne Moore

Who Were They?

Introduce your young historians to George Washington and Abraham Lincoln by showing them a picture of each man. Explain that these two men were great American presidents. Share some facts about each man (right); then tell students that we honor these two respected men on a special day called Presidents' Day. Begin your class celebration with this cheerful tune.

(sung to the tune of "I'm A Little Teapot")

Washington and Lincoln.
Who were they?
Two presidents of the U.S.A.
Honest, good, and true,
They led the way.
We honor them on Presidents' Day!

George Washington
- Born in a farmhouse on February 22, 1732
- Enjoyed riding horses and learning math
- Became a soldier, then was chosen to lead the whole army
- Elected America's first president
- Lived to the age of 67
- Known as the "Father Of Our Country"

Abraham Lincoln
- Born in a log cabin on February 12, 1809
- Worked on farms and enjoyed reading
- Became a lawyer
- Elected America's 16th president
- Lived to the age of 56
- Known as "Honest Abe"

Presidents' Day Door Display

Now that youngsters know what Presidents' Day is all about, invite them to create this patriotic display to announce this special day to others. To prepare, enlarge the silhouette patterns (page 23) on tagboard; then cut around each head outline. Trace each cutout onto a sheet of black construction paper; then cut it out. Show your class the silhouettes; then invite each child to make his own silhouette.

Have each child sit in a chair between the wall and a light source, such as a filmstrip projector or lamp. Use chalk to trace the shadow of his head onto black construction paper. Then help each child carefully cut out his silhouette. To create the display, mount the presidents' silhouettes on a door covered with white paper. Title the display "Hip, Hip, Hooray! It's Presidents' Day!" Then arrange your students' silhouettes on the door. Border the entire display with red, white, and blue streamers. For fun, challenge youngsters to identify each child's silhouette; then label each one with the child's name.

The Father Of Our Country

Why is George Washington known as the "Father Of Our Country"? Invite students to explore this reference to our first president. Read *A Picture Book Of George Washington* by David A. Adler (Holiday House); then discuss with your class what the phrase "Father Of Our Country" might mean. Ask students to brainstorm qualities of a good father, such as "he loves his children" and "he works hard for his family." Write their responses on a sheet of chart paper, leaving a space between each response. Then revisit each quality, encouraging students to tell how Washington might have acted in a similar way toward the American people. Record students' responses below each listed quality. Then conclude your discussion with a spirited round of this song.

(sung to the tune of "Do You Know The Muffin Man?")

Oh, do you know George Washington,
George Washington, George Washington?
Oh, do you know George Washington?
The Father Of Our Country!

He served as our first president,
First president, first president.
He served as our first president.
The Father Of Our Country!

Fathers love their children.
George loved the U.S.A.

Fathers work.
George worked.

Fathers protect their children.
George protected our country.

Kayla's Hat

I have **balloons** in my hat.

Lincoln's Hat

Most likely, youngsters recognize Abraham Lincoln by his stovepipe hat, but they might be surprised to learn that he used his hat for more than just covering his head! To prepare for this activity, duplicate a class supply of the hat pattern on page 23 on white paper. Then make a few tagboard tracers of the same pattern. Read *Abe Lincoln's Hat* by Martha Brenner (Random House) to acquaint youngsters with Abraham Lincoln—and his handy hat habits. Afterward, ask each child to imagine she owns a tall, black hat. What would she keep in it?

Have each student cut out her copy of the hat pattern. Ask her to illustrate one or more items that she might put in her hat; then write her dictation on the blank line. Have her trace around a tagboard hat on black construction paper, then cut out the pattern. Help each child staple her cutout over her illustration; then have her write "[Child's name]'s Hat" on the cover with chalk. During group time, invite each child to give the class a peek into her hat as she tells about its contents. Then encourage her to take her hat home to share her knowledge about Abraham Lincoln with her family.

Presidential Portraits

Capture the likenesses of any future presidents in your class with these paper-plate portraits. To prepare, supply your art center with six-inch paper plates; People Colors® markers; and an assortment of craft items such as buttons, yarn, and paper scraps. Then show your class pictures of George Washington and Abraham Lincoln. Explain that an official *portrait,* or picture, has been made of each president. Invite each child to visit your art center to create her own self-portrait. Then ask her to imagine that she is the president of the United States. What would she say to the nation? Have her write/dictate a presidential statement on a speech-bubble cutout. Then display each child's portrait and speech bubble with the title "Presidential Portraits."

Patriotic Wind Catchers

These wind catchers will have youngsters cheering Washington; Lincoln; and the red, white, and blue! To make one, cut out a copy of each of the silhouette patterns on page 23. Color each silhouette black; then glue each cutout to the back of a separate six-inch paper plate. Use red and blue markers to decorate the plate rims. Then glue 24-inch lengths of red, white, and blue crepe-paper streamers to the undecorated side of one plate. Staple the two plates together with the silhouettes facing outward. Punch two holes through the plate rims opposite the streamers; then thread a length of red yarn through the holes to create a hanger. Invite each child to take her wind catcher home and tell her family all about George Washington and Abraham Lincoln.

Patriotic Pudding Parfaits

Invite small groups of children to create these tasty pudding parfaits to wrap up your Presidents' Day celebration.

Patriotic Pudding Parfaits
(makes eight 1/4-cup servings)

1 small box of instant vanilla pudding
2 cups milk
blue food coloring

8 flat-bottomed ice-cream cones
whipped topping
frozen whole strawberries

Thaw the strawberries. Pour the milk and pudding mix into a clear quart jar. Add food coloring; then screw on the jar lid. Invite children to take turns shaking the jar for two minutes. (If needed, add more food coloring until the desired shade of blue is achieved.) Refrigerate the pudding for five minutes or until set. Spoon pudding into each cone. Add a dollop of whipped topping; then top with a strawberry. Mmm…tastes presidential!

Use with "Presidents' Day Door Display" on page 20 and "Patriotic Wind Catchers" on page 22.

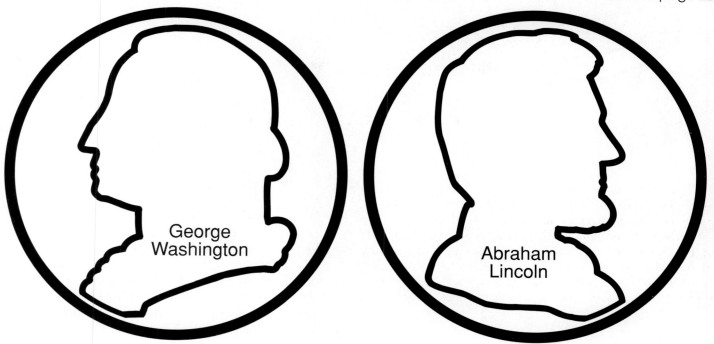

George
Washington

Abraham
Lincoln

Hat Pattern

Use with "Lincoln's Hat" on page 21.

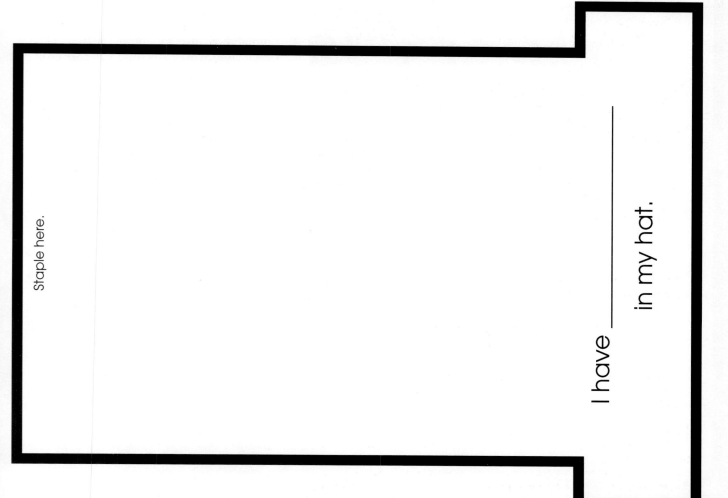

Staple here.

I have _____ in my hat.

Have A Heart

Hearts will beat wildly as your little cupids put their hearts and souls into these Valentine's Day activities.

ideas contributed by dayle timmons

Matchmakers

Set up this "valen-tastic" matching center for your little heartthrobs. Purchase six different packages of valentine cards that have different card designs centered around a theme, such as teddy bears, dinosaurs, or specific cartoon characters. Collect a card pair of each design; then store them in a large, empty valentine candy box. (Save the remaining cards for another activity.) Have each child who visits this center sort the valentines and pair each matching set. Vary the activity by inviting each child to sort the valentines by theme, resulting in larger sets of cards. Matchmaker, matchmaker, make me a match…

Heart-To-Heart Math

Your students will love this one-to-one correspondence activity! Collect pink or red dessert plates; then program each plate with a numeral. Provide a container of heart-shaped beads or seasonal erasers for counters. To use this center, have little ones place the plates in order and then count the appropriate number of manipulatives onto each plate. Upon completion of this task, give each youngster a hug for a job well done!

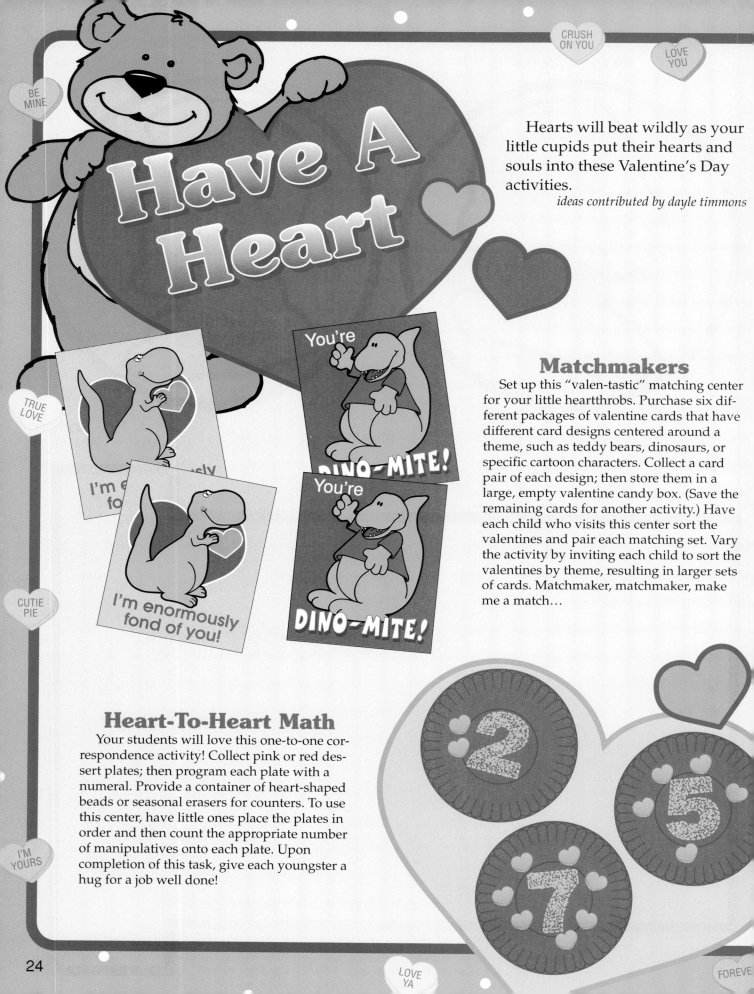

Valentine's Day "Sense-sations"

Get ready for sensory excitement with this pair of heartfelt centers!

Seeing Red?

You'll be happily seeing red when you add a few drops of red food coloring or tempera paint to your water table! When the water is the shade your heart desires, sprinkle in some glitter and foil heart-shaped confetti. Challenge each student who visits the center to either catch hearts on his hand and count them or catch a specific number of hearts. Next add measuring cups, funnels, pitchers, and spoons to the table for some sparkling exploration. What "love-ly" red water to play in!

Rosy Dough

Use more heart confetti and glitter in this sparkly sensory dough filled with valentine vim and vigor!

- 2 cups flour
- 2 cups water
- 1 cup salt
- 2 Tbs. vegetable oil
- 4 tsp. cream of tartar
- 1 small box of red gelatin

Mix the ingredients together in a medium-sized pot. Stirring constantly, cook over low heat until the dough forms a ball. Remove the dough from the heat; then knead it when it is cool. Sprinkle red glitter and confetti on your play-dough table; then place the red play dough on top. As students play with the dough, the glitter and confetti will be worked in—resulting in sparkly, rosy play dough. For more excitement, provide heart-shaped cookie cutters and interesting utensils for youngsters to use with the dough. Your little ones will see, smell, and touch red with this dazzling dough!

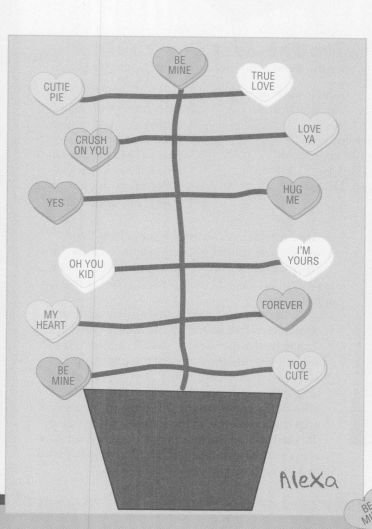

Grow A Little Love

Sow the seeds of love as you and your youngsters make these sweetie trees in your art center. For each child, gather a 4¹/₂" x 6" piece of pink construction paper, a 3" x 5" piece of red paper, red markers or crayons, and approximately 15 conversation heart candies.

To make one tree, trim the red paper into a flowerpot shape. Glue the pot at the bottom of the pink paper. Next make the tree's trunk by drawing a red line from the flowerpot toward the top of the paper. Draw horizontal lines across the trunk to resemble tree branches. When you have a desired number of branches on your tree, glue a candy conversation heart "flower" onto the end of each one. Now *that's* a sweet pot of valentine flowers!

25

A "Heart-y" Alphabet Book

Use valentine cards to create a nifty book emphasizing initial letter sounds! (If desired, use the extra cards from "Matchmakers" on page 24.) Cut 26 heart-shaped book pages from construction paper; then write one alphabet letter at the top of each page. Spread the valentine cards on the floor and place the pages nearby. Encourage children to select a valentine with a picture or word with the appropriate initial sound for each letter of the alphabet. Once a card has been chosen for each alphabet letter, have students glue each card to the matching page. Program the bottom of each page with "___ is for ___" and have students complete each sentence.

To complete the book, cut covers from tagboard. Title the front cover "Valentine Alphabet." Bind the book by folding the left side of each page to create an easily opened hinge book. Punch two holes in each page and insert brass brads. Place the finished book in your reading center for students to read. Reading through this alphabet will do your students' hearts and minds some good!

Cc
Be mine claws
I like you!
C is for cat.

Valentine Alphabet

A Valentine Just For You!

Teach your little ones the words and motions to this sweet song!

(sung to the tune of "Frère Jacques")

Valentine hearts. Valentine hearts.

Just for you. Just for you.
Sent with love and kisses.
Lots of hugs and kisses.
'Cause I love you. I love you!

Make hearts with thumbs and index fingers twice.
Point to classmates.
Hug self and throw a kiss.
Hug self and throw a kiss.
Cross hands over heart and point to classmates.

To Mommy and Daddy

Valentine hearts. Valentine hearts.
Just for you. Just for you.
Sent with love and kisses.
Lots of hugs and kisses.
'Cause I love you. I love you!

love, Allison

After teaching students the song, help them make these special pop-up valentine cards. In advance, photocopy a class supply of the song pattern on page 27 onto pink or white construction paper.

To make a card, fold a sheet of 12" x 18" red construction paper in half; then decorate it with a collage of paper hearts, doilies, and sequins. While the glue dries, cut out the photocopied song. Accordion-fold two 4" x 1" tagboard strips; then glue one end of each strip to the back of the song pattern. After the glue dries, glue the loose ends of the strips to the inside of the card so that the heart pops up when the card is opened. Encourage each child to give her card to a loved one. Happy Valentine's Day!

TOO CUTE · FOREVER · I'M YOURS · BE MINE · HUG ME · CUTIE PIE · CRUSH ON YOU · TRUE LOVE · OH YOU KID · MY HEART · YES · TOO CUTE · ALWAYS · BE MINE · LOVE YA

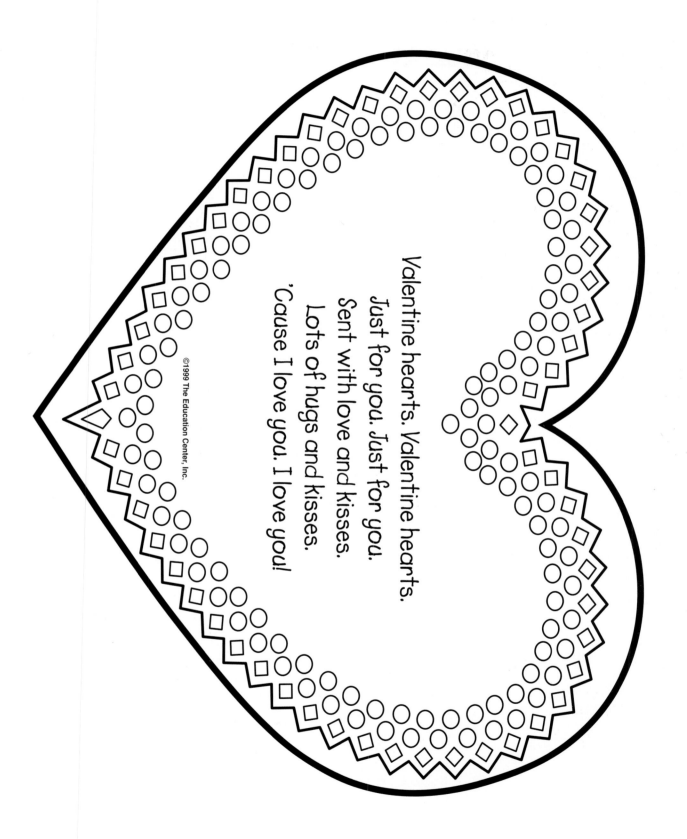

Valentine hearts. Valentine hearts.
Just for you. Just for you.
Sent with love and kisses.
Lots of hugs and kisses.
'Cause I love you. I love you!

©1999 The Education Center, Inc.

Somewhere Over The Rainbow

You won't need to go to the end of the rainbow to find St. Patrick's Day activities! Use these fresh holiday ideas that are really worth their weight in gold!

ideas contributed by Michele Dare and Chrissy Yuhouse

Who Is St. Patrick?

Introduce your class to the man behind the holiday with a discussion of St. Patrick's life. In advance, write each of the facts below on a separate shamrock cutout; then place them in a container. Have student volunteers take turns pulling a shamrock from the container. Read aloud and discuss the information on the shamrock. When all of the shamrocks have been read, mount them on a St. Patrick's day bulletin board or on a wall in your classroom. Refer to this lucky leaf display during "Plantin' Of The Green" on page 30.

St. Patrick Facts
— St. Patrick was born hundreds of years ago (around 385 A.D.)
— St. Patrick built churches and schools all over Ireland.
— Many people believe that St. Patrick planted shamrocks around Ireland and used them in his teachings.
— St. Patrick died on March 17. He was 76 years old. March 17 is now St. Patrick's Day.

I'm Lookin' Over A Four–Leaf Clover!

Don't overlook this idea: Use shamrocks for learning in your classroom! From green felt, cut sets of three- and four-leaf clovers in different sizes. Place the shamrocks in a tub near your flannelboard; then challenge your little ones to sort them, sequence them by size, or create patterns with them. To reinforce counting skills, cut individual clover leaves and stems; then invite students to create three-, four-, or even five-leaf clovers! Now *that's* lucky!

Shamrocks: Rub 'em For Luck!

Celebrate the magic of St. Patrick's Day with this amazing art activity. In advance, cut out small and large shamrock shapes from a variety of textured materials, such as sandpaper, wallpaper samples, or corduroy fabric. Or use glue to draw leaf veins on one side of a tagboard shamrock. Allow the glue to dry completely before using the shamrock for a rubbing. Tape the shamrocks, textured side up, to a table. Invite each youngster to place a sheet of paper over a shamrock and rub the side of a green glitter crayon over the clover. (If desired, help students tape their papers over the shamrocks to prevent the paper from slipping as they rub.) Wow! St. Patrick's Day magic sure does rub off on you!

Shamrock Sandwich

These delicious sandwiches are sure to satisfy even the hungriest leprechaun! To make one, spread tuna salad on a piece of bread. On top of the tuna, arrange three cucumber slices and a small slice of green pepper to resemble a three-leaf clover. Serve these sandwiches with "creamed clover" (pistachio pudding) and "leprechaun-ade" (lime-flavored punch) for a feast that will leave others green with envy!

Leapin' Leprechauns!

Your little ones will do a jig with this lively leprechaun art and movement activity! Give each child a green construction-paper hat and an orange construction-paper beard similar to those shown. Have each student glue his beard to the hat and then glue crumpled pieces of orange tissue paper to the beard. Staple the brim of the hat to a sentence strip; then adjust the strip to fit the child's head. After all of your little leprechauns have been outfitted, launch into the song and movement activity below.

I'm A Leapin' Leprechaun
(sung to the tune of "I'm A Little Teapot")

I'm a leapin' leprechaun. Watch me run!   *Run in place.*
Hiding my gold can be such fun!   *Pretend to hide gold.*
You can try to catch me if you can.   *Shake finger.*
But I'll just run away again!   *Run in place.*

Plantin' Of The Green

In addition to leaping leprechauns and magic pots of gold, St. Patrick's Day is also about honoring a man filled with kindness. Conclude your St. Patrick's Day celebration with this activity that will plant some positive seeds of learning around your school. Using the shamrock display from "Who Is St. Patrick?" (page 28), review and discuss the facts about St. Patrick. Lead your students to the conclusion that he was a kind, helpful man. After receiving approval from your school principal or director, suggest that the class plant some flowering plants around the building in honor of Ireland's patron saint. Enlist volunteers to help small groups of children with this activity. Your students will be proud of their good deed, and the legend of St. Patrick will bloom around the building year after year.

Tricked again! But take a look. It could be hidden in a book!

Go For The Gold!

Here's an activity that will have your youngsters following directions to the end of the rainbow. In advance, duplicate onto green construction paper the shamrock clues on page 31. Laminate the shamrocks; then cut them out. Keep the first shamrock with you; then hide the rest according to the directions on the previous shamrock. Invite a small group of students to join you in a search for a leprechaun's pot of gold. Begin the hunt by reading the first shamrock to the children. When they find the second shamrock, read the clue that directs them to the third shamrock. Continue in this manner until the final shamrock has been read and the children have found the leprechaun's treasure—a basket full of gold foil-wrapped chocolate coins. Celebrate by giving each child in the group a coin to eat; then repeat the game with another small group of children. What a 24-karat idea!

Shamrock Clues

Use with "Go For The Gold!" on page 30.

I am a leprechaun and it's been told.
I like to hide my pot of gold.
Some gold you will find without a care
If you look under a chair!

1

Oops! No gold here!
I have fooled you all!
Now try looking in the hall!

2

Tricked again! But take a look.
It could be hidden in a book!

3

If you want my treasure
And you are able,
Take a peek under a table!

4

Tricked again and fooled once more!
Now try looking on the floor!

5

This is my final clue to you
So I will tell you what to do.
Look up, down, all around.
Now quietly without a sound,
Search the room until you see
The pot of gold hidden by me!

6

The Easter Boutique

Shopping for some new ideas for Easter? Then grab your Easter basket and hop on into this unit for a unique collection of holiday treats and eats.

ideas contributed by Deborah Garmon

A Cute Little Bunny

Ask youngsters to hop on over to circle time to learn this fingerplay about a chance meeting with a bunny.

I looked in the garden,
And what did I see?
A cute little bunny
Peeking at me.
I bent down to pat him.
Then he hopped away.
I hope he comes back
To see me someday!

Shade eyes with hand.
Hold out hands and shrug shoulders.
Make rabbit ears with hands.

Pretend to pat bunny.
Hop two fingers away.
Clasp hands in front of chest.
Use thumb to point to self.

Bunny See, Bunny Do

Invite your busy little bunnies to develop their spatial awareness with this idea. To begin, have each child create a bunny-ear headband from construction paper. Have youngsters don their headbands; then divide your class into student pairs. Instruct one child in each pair to assume the role of the Easter Bunny. Have him strike a pose; then ask his partner to imitate the pose. After several rounds, have the partners switch roles and continue play. When interest begins to wane, have your bunny-eared students line up for a rambunctious romp to "The Bunny Hop" or "Here Comes Peter Cottontail."

Rabbit Recall

Challenge your youngsters' visual memory with a game of Rabbit Recall. In advance, duplicate two sets of the rabbit cards on page 35. (You might duplicate four sets for more advanced students.) Cut out each card; then glue a 2 1/2-inch square of seasonal gift wrap onto the back of each one. Laminate the cards for durability. To play, place all the cards facedown. Have student pairs play Rabbit Recall following the rules of Memory. After the pair finds all the matches, invite another student pair to play.

Easter Eats

Your little Easter bunnies will "hop-pily" return for seconds—and thirds—of this delicious dish with a nutritious twist! To make one serving, grate half of a carrot into a clear plastic cup. Count out up to ten raisins and ten mini marshmallows; then add them to the grated carrots. Stir in some vanilla yogurt. Then invite youngsters to wear their headbands from "Bunny See, Bunny Do" (page 32) as they nibble away at their special treats.

A Pretty Easter Basket

A-tisket, a-tasket, what a pretty Easter basket! Youngsters will be just as happy with these baskets as they will be with the contents! To create one, tear an assortment of seasonal gift wrap into small pieces. Then paint the inside of a Styrofoam® bowl with water-thinned glue. Glue the torn paper along the bottom and inner walls of the bowl, allowing the stray edges to extend over the rim. After the glue dries, attach a pipe-cleaner handle to the basket. Line the bottom of each child's basket with Easter grass. Then invite youngsters to use their baskets during a class egg hunt. Or fill each basket with Easter goodies and party favors.

The Easter Egg Trail

Youngsters will happily hop into this sweet color-recognition game. To prepare, cut one small and one large egg shape from each of several colors of construction paper. Laminate the large eggs for durability. Then attach each small egg to a paper bag. Partially fill each bag with individually wrapped Easter candies. Tape the large eggs onto the floor in a large oval shape.

To play, students pretend to be bunnies. They hop around the oval as you sing the song below. On the word *stop*, each bunny stands on an egg. The child named tells the color of his egg. Then he picks a treat from the bag labeled with the corresponding color. That child sits out and sings along as a new round is played. Continue until all the bunnies have had a turn to pick a treat from a bag. Then invite all your bunnies to nibble their sweet treats.

(sung to the tune of "Pop Goes The Weasel")

All around the Easter egg trail
We hop on every color.
Stop and look at the egg that you're on.
[Child's name], name your color.

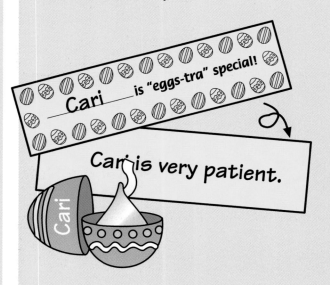

"Eggs-tra" Special Eggs

Here's a neat way to let youngsters know that they are "eggs-tra" special. Using paint pens, decorate and label a separate plastic egg for each child; then duplicate and cut out a supply of the student note on page 35. Write a note to each child, praising a positive character trait or noting a positive action you observe. Roll up the note and put it in her egg, along with a piece of Hershey's® Kisses® or Hershey's® Hugs® candy. Place the egg in the child's Easter basket or goodie bag. This "eggs-tra" touch is guaranteed to make youngsters feel "eggs-traordinarily" special!

"Sense-ational" Eggs

Youngsters will employ all their senses when they mix up these tasty Easter treats. Ask students to help you combine a medium-sized jar of creamy peanut butter with one-fourth cup of honey. Then add nonfat dry milk until the mixture has the consistency of play dough. Give each child a small amount of the peanut-butter dough and a speckled malted candy egg. Have him mold the dough into an egg shape around the candy; then invite him to roll his egg in seasonal cake sprinkles. Finally—*crunch!*—invite youngsters to enjoy these tasty treats. They're simply "sense-ational"!

_____ is "eggs-tra" special!

Passover

Use this collection of activities to teach your youngsters about the history and traditions of this ancient Jewish holiday.

Passover Fast Facts

- Passover celebrates the ancient Jews' deliverance from Egyptian slavery.
- It is celebrated by more Jews than any other Jewish holiday.
- It begins on the 15th day of Nisan (late March–mid April).
- Most Jews celebrate Passover for eight days.

The Seder Plate

Begin your Passover study by discussing the foods that make up the traditional Seder meal. Each food represents a different aspect of the Jews' flight from Egypt (see "Seder Plate Foods"). Then have students complete the following matching activity.

To prepare, copy onto white construction paper two sets of the Seder food cards (page 39). Color and cut out the cards. Laminate one set of cards and set it aside. Glue the other set of cards onto a paper plate as shown. To represent the dishes on a Seder plate, glue a cupcake liner next to each Seder food card. To play, a child places each laminated card in the cupcake liner with the matching card. For an added challenge, have each child name each Seder food. Vary this activity by making only one set of Seder food cards. Glue six cupcake liners to a paper plate; then label each liner with a different Seder food. To play, a child places each card into the matching muffin-liner dish.

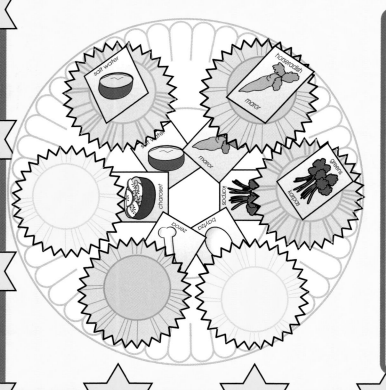

Seder Plate Foods

- *Maror* (bitter herbs, often horseradish) represents the Jewish people's bitter lot in Egypt.
- *Karpas* (fresh greens, such as parsley or celery leaves) symbolizes springtime and rebirth.
- *Salt water* represents the salty tears shed by the Jews. The *karpas* is dipped in salt water before it is eaten.
- *Charoset* (an apple-nut mixture) symbolizes the mortar Jews made during slavery.
- *Zeroa* (roasted bone) is a symbol of the lamb the Israelites cooked and ate on the night they fled Egypt.
- *Baytza* (roasted, hard-boiled egg) is a symbol of life and also represents the festival offerings of ancient times.

Recline Time

When the Jewish people were enslaved in Egypt, they worked hard all day, every day; and they did not have the freedom to stop working and rest when they needed to. Now it is a Passover tradition to place cushions and pillows in chairs so that people may relax. This symbolizes freedom and independence. Invite groups of students to help make cushions for the classroom. For each cushion cover, obtain a 1' x 2' piece of white or light-colored fabric. Fold the fabric in half to make a square; then close two of the remaining three sides by sewing or by using fabric glue. Slip a sheet of cardboard inside the cushion cover to provide support and prevent color transfer while decorating.

Have each group decorate a cushion with fabric crayons or markers (set the colors according to package directions). Remove the cardboard and stuff each cushion with polyester batting or craft filling; then sew or glue the cushion closed. Place the cushions in your class library or a quiet classroom area for some well-deserved relaxation!

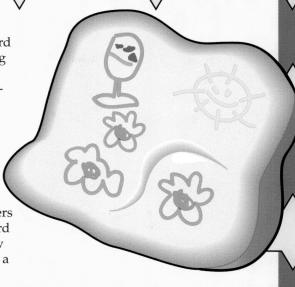

Lotsa Matzoh

Your little ones are sure to enjoy this jolly tune about Passover's unleavened bread! After a rousing rendition, serve everyone a treat—matzoh with butter and jam!

(sung to the tune of "Are You Sleeping?")
Lotsa matzoh,
Lotsa matzoh,
Fun to eat
Passover treat.
Flat and crunchy bread.
Flat and crunchy bread.
Matzoh munch!
Matzoh munch!

An Artistic Afikomon Cloth

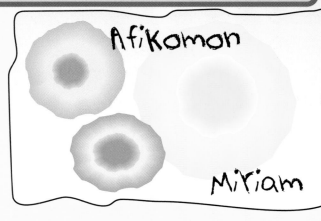

Near the beginning of the Seder service, a special piece of matzoh called an *afikomon* is wrapped in a cloth or bag. In some families, the afikomon is hidden and children search for it. When the afikomon is found, the Seder leader breaks it into pieces to share with each person at the table. These tie-dyed afikomon cloths will lend an extra special touch to your Passover study.

In advance, prepare a few different colors of commercial fabric dyes, or make your own by combining one-half cup water and seven or eight drops of food coloring for each desired color. To make one tie-dyed afikomon cloth, write "Afikomon" and your name on a plain white cotton handkerchief (or square of cotton cloth) with a fabric marker. Twist the cloth and secure it in several areas with rubber bands. Dip different areas of the cloth into the dyes. Remove the rubber bands and lay the cloth flat to dry. Encourage students to take their afikomon cloths home to use during their Seder feasts. If you have students that do not celebrate Passover, suggest they use their cloths to cover the breadbasket at family meals.

Seder Cups

Each person participating in the Seder feast has a special cup to use during the meal. Invite each youngster to decorate his own cup using this simple technique. Purchase a classroom quantity of clear, plastic wineglasses. Using a permanent marker, personalize a cup for each child. With his cup turned upside down on a table, instruct the child to use fabric paints to decorate the bowl of the cup. After the paint is dry, use these hand-decorated cups in a classroom Seder feast (see "Let's Feast!").

Charoset

(Makes approximately 24 quarter-cup servings)
4 medium apples, quartered and cored
1 cup chopped walnuts
2 teaspoons cinnamon
2 tablespoons honey
4 tablespoons grape juice

Finely chop the apple pieces. In a large bowl, combine the chopped apple, walnuts, and cinnamon. Mix in the honey, then the grape juice. Refrigerate the mixture for an hour to allow the flavors to blend.

Mmm—Charoset

Charoset is a sweet dish made of apples, nuts, and other ingredients that is served during Passover. It is served during the Seder feast to represent the mortar Jewish people made while they were enslaved in Egypt. To bring a taste of Passover to your classroom, provide students with plastic knives and invite them to help make this version of charoset.

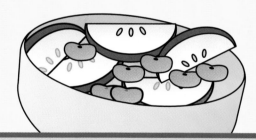

Let's Feast!

Culminate your Passover unit with this classroom version of a Seder feast. In advance, wrap a piece of matzoh in a tie-dyed afikomon cloth (see page 37) and hide it. Serve each child grape juice in her specially decorated cup (see "Seder Cups"). Also give each child small servings of charoset and matzah. When the children have finished eating, invite them to hunt for the afikomon. What a special ending for your Passover unit!

More Passover Stories

Use these easy-to-understand and entertaining stories to extend youngsters' learning about Passover.

Passover Magic
Written by Roni Schotter
Published by Little, Brown and Company

Sammy Spider's First Passover
Written by Sylvia A. Rouss
Published by Kar-Ben Copies

Matzo Ball Moon
Written by Leslea Newman
Published by Clarion Books

egg

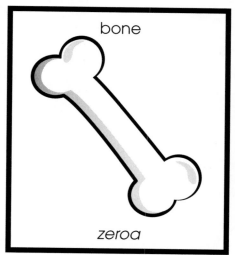

baytza

bone

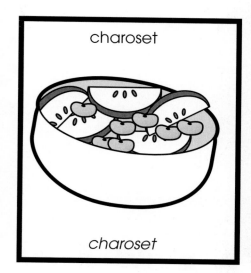

zeroa

charoset

charoset

horseradish

maror

salt water

greens

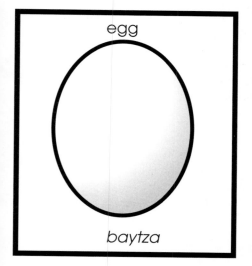

karpas

Happy Earth Day To You!

Celebrate Earth Day with these awesome ideas, and your little environmentalists will soon understand that the whole world is in their hands.

ideas contributed by Suzanne Moore

Start With A Story

What is Earth Day all about? Explain to your youngsters that it's a day set aside to remind everyone to take good care of our earth. Share *The Earth And I* by Frank Asch (Harcourt Brace & Company), a story that illustrates in simple terms the important relationship between the earth and humankind. Afterward, ask youngsters to make a list of things that they think make the earth sad and a list of things that they think make the earth happy. Record the lists on a chart as shown. Then reinforce some happy earth practices with the following song:

I'm Giving The Earth Just What It Needs
(sung to the tune of "I'm A Little Teapot")

Taking care of the earth is good to do.
It's home to plants and animals, too.
When I pick up trash or pull some weeds,
I'm giving the earth just what it needs.

I need to think before I throw away.
Can I use something another way?
I can use a box to hold my beads.
I'm giving the earth just what it needs.

I care for the earth and its critters, too.
Planting a tree is good to do.
When I feed a bird or plant some seeds,
I'm giving the earth just what it needs.

sad	happy
too much trash dirty water dirty air from cars	picking up trash planting flowers feeding birds

A Whole Lot Of Garbage Going On

These handy trash bags will help your little ones see just how much garbage they produce in one day. To make a trash bag, a child colors a copy of the earth pattern on page 43 and then cuts it out. He glues the pattern to one side of a paper lunch bag, then uses markers, crayons, or colorful paper scraps to decorate around the earth. Then he folds down the top of his decorated bag a few times.

Ask students to use their bags as their own personal trash cans for the day, throwing in paper scraps, food wrappers, and other trash. (Since students will handle their trash later, ask them to throw used tissues, bandages, or other unsanitary items in your *classroom* trash can.) Near the end of the day, have each student empty his bag onto a newspaper-covered surface. Lead a discussion of different ways some of the trashed items might be reused. Then invite each student to create a garbage collage by gluing some of his trash onto a sheet of construction paper. And don't trash those paper bag trash cans! Have students take them home to use in their rooms or in their parents' cars.

No-Trash Snack

One look at your classroom trash can after lunch or snacktime, and it's obvious that many food items are overpackaged. Help your youngsters learn to reduce and reuse with this snack idea. Before snacktime one day, ask students what the term *waste-free* means. After discussing student ideas, tell youngsters that they will be preparing a snack where nothing will be thrown away. Bring out a tray with a class supply of flour tortillas, a tub of cream cheese, and a few butter knives. Ask students to think of new classroom uses for the plastic bags from the tortillas and the plastic tub from the cream cheese. Then invite small groups of students to prepare this earth-friendly snack by spreading cream cheese onto tortillas, then rolling them up to eat. When snacktime's over, encourage students to help you wash the containers and put them to use in your classroom.

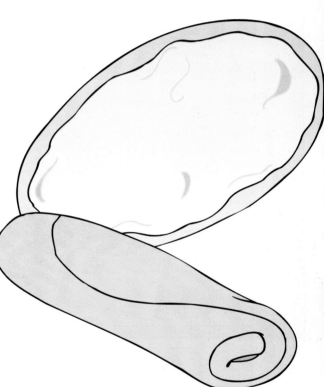

One Man's Trash...

...can be your treasure when you reuse throwaway items in your classroom centers. And what better time than Earth Day to add a few new items! Here are some ideas:

- Cut the lids from several egg cartons; then use the bottoms for sorting trays.
- Make weights for scale comparisons by filling film canisters with sand. Hot-glue the lids in place.
- Fill your sensory table with Styrofoam® packing pieces or shredded paper.
- Stuff empty cardboard food containers with newspaper. Seal the boxes with clear tape; then place them in your dramatic-play area.
- Stuff empty tissue boxes with newspaper. Then secure the openings with clear tape and add these to your block center.

A Helping Hand

Earth Day reminds us that the future of the earth is in our hands. Encourage your little ones to think of different ways they can give the earth and its creatures a helping hand; then create this "hand-some" display. Duplicate the poster pattern on page 43 for each child. Have each child complete the speech bubble by writing or dictating a way he can care for the earth. Have him glue a photo of himself in the space provided, and then glue the pattern to the bottom of a 9" x 12" sheet of blue construction paper. Complete the poster by having each child press his hand into green tempera paint, then onto his poster as shown. To create a display, enlarge a copy of the earth pattern on page 43 and color it. Mount the earth pattern on a bulletin-board background; then staple the helping-hand posters around the earth. Title the display "We're Giving The Earth A Helping Hand."

Earth-Friendly Literature Links

Someday A Tree
Written by Eve Bunting
Published by Clarion Books

Hey! Get Off Our Train
Written by John Burningham
Published by Crown Publishers, Inc.

The Lorax
Written by Dr. Seuss
Published by Random House, Inc.

Dinosaurs To The Rescue!
Written by Laurie Krasny Brown and Marc Brown
Published by Little, Brown and Company

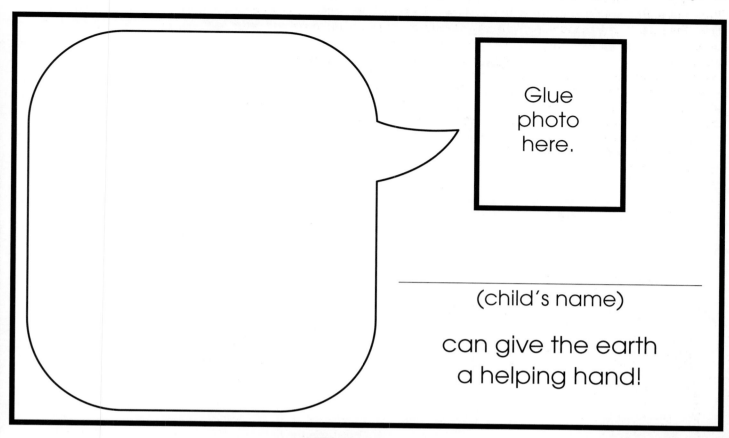

Glue
photo
here.

_____

(child's name)

can give the earth
a helping hand!

Earth Pattern
Use with "A Whole Lot Of Garbage
Going On" on page 41 and
"A Helping Hand" on page 42.

A "Kinder-garden" Gala

Kindergarten Day is April 21, the birthday of Friedrich Froebel. Born in Germany in 1782, Froebel was one founder of schools designed for very young children. To name these schools, he coined the German term *kindergarten,* which means "a garden of children." He wanted to convey the idea that young children should grow and learn freely, like plants in a garden.

So, what better way to celebrate Kindergarten Day than with these ideas guaranteed to help your garden grow? Help little ones learn about plant growth, then reflect on their own growth. Culminate your unit with fresh-picked ideas for a garden party!

ideas contributed by Kristin Bauer Ganoung

> Before our trip, we think plants need:
>
> • dirt
> • pots
> • water

> After our trip, we know plants need:
>
> • dirt
> • air
> • water
> • sun
> • some bugs

How Does Your Garden Grow?

Introduce your little gardeners to plant care by taking a field trip to a local greenhouse, garden center, or nearby backyard garden (with a knowledgeable resident gardener). In advance, involve students in a class discussion about plant care. Record students' responses on a chart as they describe how gardeners care for plants, as well as what tools and supplies gardeners use.

While on the field trip, ask a gardener to demonstrate potting (or planting bedding plants), and to explain how the plants are cared for. Have youngsters observe the types of tools, supplies, and plants.

Upon returning to school, ask the children to share their observations. Encourage youngsters to recall the tools and materials that the gardeners used to care for the plants. Write the responses on a second chart; then compare them to the first chart. Refer to this set of charts throughout your garden unit to reinforce students' understanding of plant care and growth.

Green Thumb Central

Are your little ones sprouting green thumbs? They *will* be once they explore this down-and-dirty garden store! In advance, stock your dramatic-play area or discovery center with tubs of potting soil, a class supply of personalized small flowerpots (or use empty milk cartons or paper cups), artificial flowers, and packets of easy-to-grow seeds such as marigolds, beans, zinnias, or corn. Also supply gloves and plastic gardening tools. If you used the idea described above (in "How Does Your Garden Grow?"), place the resulting charts in the center for easy reference.

Invite each child in this center to take turns pretending to be a gardener and a customer. Encourage students in the store to care for any sprouted plants as needed. Have students measure and record plant growth, as well as experiment with the amounts of water and light plants are given. Leave this center in place for a few weeks. Before long, your classroom will resemble Froebel's garden—children and plants growing freely!

What Do We Need To Grow?

Your youngsters understand that plants need water, light, and soil to grow. But do they know what *they* need to grow? Read aloud Demi's *The Empty Pot* (Henry Holt And Company, Inc.), which tells how Ping tried to make a special seed grow but failed. After a shared reading of this charming tale, discuss with students how Ping learned and grew even though his seed did not. Explain that people grow in two different ways—on the outside, like plants, and on the inside, by learning new things.

Try this display idea to illustrate the concept of growing on the inside and on the outside. Cut out two large flowerpot shapes from bulletin-board paper. Label one cutout "plants" and the other "people." Mount both cutouts on a bulletin board covered in brightly colored paper. As you write on the cutout labeled "plants," encourage students to name what plants need to grow. Next have volunteers draw and cut out construction-paper plants. Attach the plants to the bulletin board so they appear to grow from the pot. Repeat this activity with the cutout labeled "people," making sure to include important things like love, good books, food, and shelter. Then have each child draw a small self-portrait, and arrange the portraits so they appear to grow from the pot. This display will make it easy for little ones to explain to visitors what they need to grow.

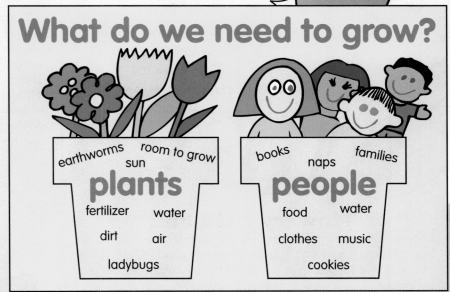

What do we need to grow?

plants
earthworms room to grow
sun
fertilizer water
dirt air
ladybugs

people
books families
naps
food water
clothes music
cookies

That's "Kinder-tainment"!

Sum up a year's worth of kindergarten in one fun swoop with this sensational song! To begin, brainstorm things your students have learned this year, such as their ABCs, the Pledge of Allegiance, and colors. Then lead youngsters in a song verse for each accomplishment. What a jolly way to let your students show off all they have learned this year!

(sung to the tune of "If You're Happy And You Know It")

If you've grown some this year, clap your hands.
If you've grown some this year, clap your hands.
If you've grown some this year, clap your hands and give a cheer!
If you've grown some this year, clap your hands.

If you've [learned your ABCs], clap your hands.
If you've [learned your ABCs], clap your hands.
If you've [learned your ABCs], clap your hands and give a cheer!
If you've [learned your ABCs], clap your hands.

Continue with additional verses as desired.

Gardener's Almanac

Now that your youngsters realize they are growing and changing every day, have each child record some of his growth in an almanac, just as gardeners do. For each child, make one copy of the cover and several copies of the booklet page on page 47. To complete each booklet page, have the child illustrate a task she can now perform, but was unable to do before kindergarten began. Encourage her to complete the sentence (or dictate a sentence ending for you to write) to describe the task. When she has completed the booklet pages, have her illustrate the cover, including a self-portrait in the center of the flower. Help her stack the pages behind the cover and staple the booklet on the left side. Read each child's booklet aloud; then display the booklets in your classroom library. Your little growers will enjoy reading about all the new accomplishments!

45

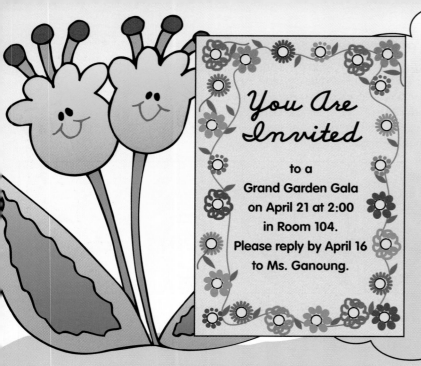

You Are
Invited

to a
Grand Garden Gala
on April 21 at 2:00
in Room 104.
Please reply by April 16
to Ms. Ganoung.

Come One, Come All!

Wrap up your Kindergarten Day celebration with a garden party! Have each child make his family a festive, flowery invitation. To make one invitation, give the child a 9" x 12" sheet of construction paper and access to a hole puncher. Have him punch well-spaced holes around the edges of the paper to create a border. Next have him glue a yellow sheet of 9" x 12" construction paper behind the first sheet, so the yellow shows through the holes. Instruct the youngster to use markers to draw flower petals around each yellow center, as shown. Encourage him to add leaves and connecting vines to complete the border. Help the child write a message (similar to the one shown) in the center of the paper, inviting his family to the garden gala. When the invitation is complete, ask the child to deliver it to his family.

Flowery Food Fun

Not only is this tantalizing array of edible botanicals tasty, but it provides patterning and fine-motor practice, too! Before guests arrive for your garden party, have youngsters use plastic knives to help section or slice a variety of fruits and vegetables, such as kiwi, oranges, strawberries, grapes, celery, cucumbers, and carrots. Arrange the pieces on platters along with bowls of fruit and vegetable dip. If you are expecting a large number of guests, consider setting up two snack areas to ease traffic flow.

When your guests arrive, invite them to assemble edible flowers from the available ingredients, creating simple patterns with the petals (see the illustration). If desired, encourage partygoers to display their creations before devouring them. My, what a delicious garden!

A Grand Garden Gala

Of course there's more to this garden party than a yummy snack! Have each student greet the guests, then escort her family around the classroom. Encourage each child to read her booklet with her family (see page 45), show off the garden store (see "Green Thumb Central" on page 44), and explain the bulletin-board display (see page 45). Then have the class sing several verses of the song (from "That's 'Kinder-tainment'!" on page 45). And be sure to serve your favorite punch with the edible flowers described in "Flowery Food Fun." What a grand way to celebrate Kindergarten Day!

Now I Can!

When I was small, I couldn't...

Now I can!

Let's Celebrate May Day!

On the first of May, welcome the arrival of spring with this fun-filled outdoor celebration! Use these ideas and activities to organize a May Day festival that will thrill your little fairies and sprites!

ideas contributed by Mimi Duffy

Signs Of Spring

Blue skies; red robins; and yellow, pink, and purple flowers! Begin your May Day festivities by taking your youngsters on a nature walk around the school to observe the vibrant colors of spring. When you return to the classroom, have your little ones recall the many different colors of the new season. Next invite each child to finger-paint a large sheet of paper with one of the season's colors. When the paint is dry, help him cut the paper into the shape of a flower, a leaf, a bird, or another springtime object. Mount each child's painting on a bulletin board to create a colorful May Day display.

A-Tisket, A-Tasket...

...a pretty May Day basket! Use this charming basket to invite parents and staff members to a May Day celebration. To make a basket, use watercolors to paint flowers on the back side of a white paper plate. When the paint is dry, fold the plate into a cone shape and glue the edges together. Punch a hole in each side of the basket's top; then twist a pipe cleaner through the holes for a handle. Next glue small construction-paper leaves on the basket. Duplicate the invitation and the RSVP card on page 51. Color them; then cut them out. Punch a hole in the top of the card and tie it to the handle with curling ribbon. Finally, fill the basket with small treats, fresh or tissue-paper flowers, and the invitation. In keeping with May Day tradition, have small groups of children deliver baskets to staff members by knocking on a recipient's door and then quickly leaving a basket without being seen. Good work, little sprites!

RSVP
☑ I will attend the festival.
☐ I am unable to attend the festival.
Virginia Hardee

May Day Kings And Queens

Dress your little ones for the occasion by having your boys wear crowns of leaves and your girls wear crowns of flowers. To make one of these May Day headpieces, cut out the center of a large, white paper plate; then paint the remaining rim green. When the paint is dry, glue tissue-paper flowers or construction-paper leaves on the crown. Add a construction-paper butterfly to the flowers or a construction-paper ladybug to the leaves. As a finishing touch, glue two lengths of streamers to the back of the crown. Have your little ones wear these headpieces as they parade through the school gathering guests for your May Day festival (see "A Perfect Parade").

A Perfect Parade

When the sun approaches high noon, get ready to celebrate May Day or go a-maying. Have students wear their crowns (see "May Day Kings And Queens") and begin a May Day parade through your school. If desired, provide each child with a small musical instrument to play, such as a bell or a pair of rhythm sticks. Have your little ones sing the song below as they invite guests to join the parade and follow them out to the celebration site.

Here We Go A-Maying

(sung to the tune of "The Mulberry Bush")

Here we go a-maying,
A-maying, a-maying.
Here we go a-maying
On the first of May.

Wearing leaves and flowers,
Flowers, flowers.
Wearing leaves and flowers
On the first of May.

Come and join the party,
The party, the party.
Come and join the party
To welcome in this May.

49

Shall We Dance?

No Mayfest would be complete without a little dancing! If your school has a tall, sturdy pole, have students perform a traditional Maypole dance. If not, have students use their imaginations to create their own dance. Have your little ones form a circle; then provide each child with a streamer. Play a lively musical selection and direct students to move creatively around the circle, waving their streamers to the music.

Flower Relay

After the dance, continue the festivities with this exciting relay race. In advance, cut out a class supply of construction-paper flowers. Laminate the flowers; then tape a jumbo craft stick to the back of each one. For added fun, make enough flowers so that parents and other guests can also participate in the race. Divide your class and guests into teams. Place a plastic hoop for each team on the ground and then have each team line up facing its hoop. Give each relay participant a flower cutout. At the start signal, the first person in line runs to the plastic hoop and plants his flower by sticking the craft stick in the ground. He then runs back to the line and tags the next person. The race continues in this manner until all flowers have been planted. Wow! It looks like spring has sprung!

Maypole Munchies

After all that dancing and running, your little ones and guests will have worked up an appetite for this yummy Maypole snack. Have your children and guests follow the recipe below to create a springtime treat that looks *almost* too good to eat.

Ingredients for one snack:
1 cupcake
green-tinted frosting
pastel-colored sprinkles
1 Pepperidge Farm® Pirouette™ cookie
1 gumdrop
six 3" lengths of 1/8-inch-wide ribbon

Spread green-tinted frosting on the cupcake; then add sprinkles. Cover one end of the cookie with frosting, and insert the other end into the middle of the cupcake. Place the ribbons on the cookie as shown; then add a gumdrop to the top of the cookie. (Remove the ribbons before eating the cupcake.)

You are cordially invited to a May Day festival!

Please join _____'s
(teacher's name)
class on _____
(date)
at _____.
(time)
Come help us herald spring!

RSVP
☐ I will attend the festival.
☐ I am unable to attend the festival.

_____
(signature)

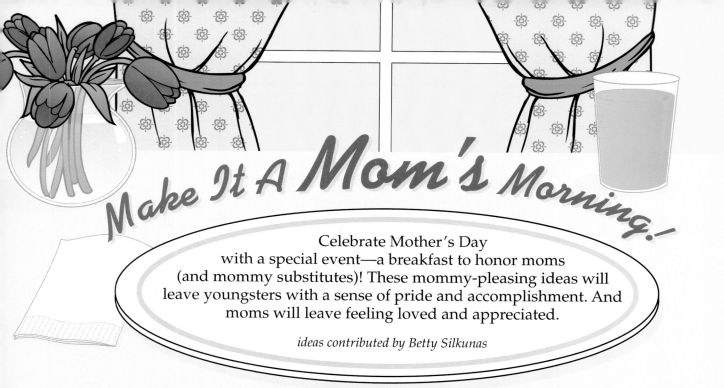

Make It A Mom's Morning!

Celebrate Mother's Day
with a special event—a breakfast to honor moms
(and mommy substitutes)! These mommy-pleasing ideas will
leave youngsters with a sense of pride and accomplishment. And
moms will leave feeling loved and appreciated.

ideas contributed by Betty Silkunas

An Important Invitation

Plan to make and send out these special invitations a couple of weeks in advance so that busy moms can schedule this event along with other important appointments. Make one copy of the invitation on page 55; then program the copy with the date, time, and place of Mom's Morning. (Leave the line for the child's name blank.) Duplicate and cut out a class supply of the programmed invitation. Give each child a copy of the cutout. Have her write her name on the blank line; then help her center and glue the invitation on a sheet of construction paper. Invite her to use markers, stickers, and glitter to decorate the construction-paper border. Then send each child home with her invitation. Such a lovely invitation is sure to capture attention and get priority booking on Mom's busy calendar.

Meet Our Moms

Have youngsters create this class banner to introduce their mothers to their classmates, then later to other moms. First title a length of bulletin-board paper "Meet Our Moms" in large bold print. Then prompt a group discussion about mothers. Ask each child to describe his mother, using words to tell about his mom's height, eye color, hairstyle, or even clothing preferences. Then ask each child to illustrate his mother on the banner. Have him label his illustration "[Child's name]'s Mom." When each student's mom is represented on the banner, invite each child to describe his mom once again, using the illustration as a visual aid. Then set the banner aside to display later during Mom's Morning.

snugglers
happy   pretty   huggers

Mothers Are...Marvelous!

Now that students have moms on their minds, direct their thoughts to all the great qualities of their mothers. Ask children to brainstorm words that describe all the different ways that their moms are special, such as "great readers," "wonderful cooks," and "cool!" List their responses on a sheet of chart paper titled "Mothers Are…" Then provide an assortment of spring-related stamps and stamp-pad colors. Invite small groups of students, in turn, to border the list with the stamps. Then put the chart away to use during Mom's Morning.

busy   super fun
good cooks   mushy
good drivers

Cool Corsages

These simple corsages are sure to bring smiles to mothers' faces. To begin, make several tagboard tracers of the leaf and flower patterns on page 55. To make a corsage, trace the leaf pattern on green construction paper and the flower pattern on pink construction paper. Cut out both patterns; then attach the flower to the leaf with a glue stick. Write each mother's name on a half-length file folder label. Help the child stick the label onto a leaf. Then add crunched-up tissue-paper petals to the flower. Place the corsages aside until the day of your special event. At that time, attach a piece of rolled tape to the back of each corsage; then invite each child to present her mother with a cool corsage.

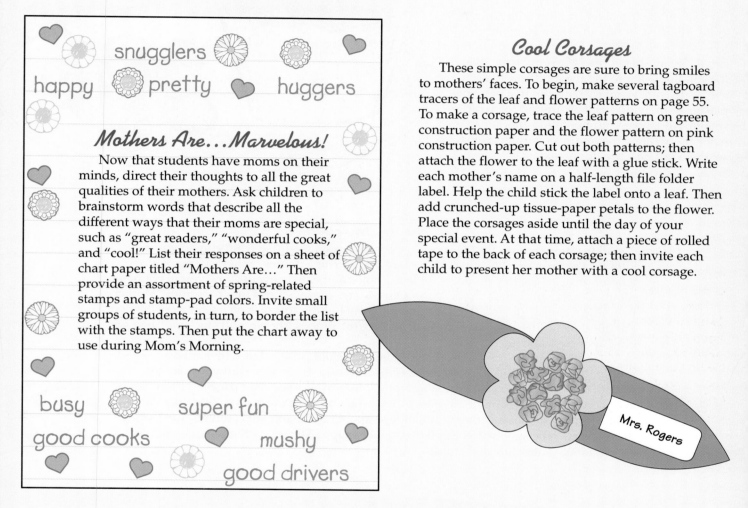

Mrs. Rogers

Mommy, It's You!

Tune youngsters in to this bouncy song that sings the praises of mommies everywhere. A few days before your big event, teach your class this song and the accompanying gestures. Then, during Mom's Morning, invite students to perform the song for their moms. On the last line of each verse, have each child point to his own mother. Afterward, send each child to his mommy to give her a huge hug.

(sung to the tune of "Santa Claus Is Coming To Town")

Who gives me a hug?
Tucks me in snug?
Squeezes me tight, then turns off the light?
Mommy, Mommy, Mommy, it's you!

Hug self.
Pull imaginary blanket up to chin.
Squeeze self; then pretend to turn off light.
Point to Mommy.

Who tickles my toes?
Helps with my clothes?
Gives me a snack and then rubs my back?
Mommy, Mommy, Mommy, it's you!

Tickle toes.
Tug at shirt.
Rub tummy; then use thumb to point over shoulder.
Point to Mommy.

Yummy Muffins For Mommy

Mommy will be pleasantly surprised when she bites into one of these muffins! On the day before your mom's breakfast, provide a box of chocolate chip muffin mix for every eight to ten students in your class. Working with one group at a time, mix up and bake the muffins according to the package directions. After the muffins are cooked and cooled, help each child carefully cut a slit in the top of one muffin with a plastic knife. Then ask her to unwrap a Hershey's® Kisses® candy. Have her insert the candy in the slit; then have her spread a layer of icing over the slit. Invite her to top the muffin with a chocolate chip. Wrap each muffin in a piece of plastic wrap, tying a ribbon around the wrap as shown. Add a tag with the child's mother's name. Refrigerate the muffins overnight; then set them out on a tray for breakfast.

The Main Event

All the preparations for the special event have been made, so what else do you need? Film for your camera, of course! Don't forget to recruit a photographer—perhaps a co-worker or a classroom volunteer—to take photos at the main event. Now you're ready to set up. Display the banner from "Meet Our Moms" (page 52) and the chart from "Mothers Are…Marvelous!" (page 53) in prominent places. Put the corsages on a table near the door. Put out the muffins along with trays of sliced fruit, grapes, cheese, and crackers. Then set out paper cups and juice.

As mothers arrive for the breakfast, have each child present her with her corsage and muffin. Invite the moms to serve themselves food and drink. When all your mothers are settled, have youngsters sing the song from "Mommy, It's You!" on page 53. Then encourage each child to show off her mommy illustration on the banner, as well as visit the chart with her mom so that together they can read about how marvelous mothers are. During the celebration be sure that your photographer snaps a shot of each mom-and-child pair (or each mom substitute and child).

Mom's Morning Mementos

Even though the big event may be over, the excitement can linger long afterwards with these special mementos. After you develop the photos from Mom's Morning, show each child the picture of him with his mother. Ask him to dictate a special message to his mom. Write his dictation on a speech bubble in the shape of a heart. Then help him mount the photo and the speech bubble on a half sheet of construction paper. Laminate each child's memento; then attach a piece of magnetic tape to the back of it. Send each child's memento home with him to display on his family's refrigerator as a special reminder of a special event for a special mom!

We're Making It
A Mom's Morning!

Please join us for a special celebration to honor our moms.

When?_____

What time? _____

Where? _____

Why? Because_____ loves you!

Leaf And Flower Patterns
Use with "Cool Corsages" on page 53.

A Day For Dads

Father's Day is celebrated on the third Sunday in June. Use the ideas in this unit to get youngsters thinking about this important family role and to create some memorable gifts that dads will treasure.

ideas contributed by Carol Plaut

Dads Are...

What are the qualities that make a dad special? Invite each child in your class to give her own unique answer to this question when you create a poster honoring dads. At the top of a sheet of chart paper, write "Dads Are..." Then ask the children to brainstorm descriptive words and phrases to finish that thought. Record their responses on the chart paper. Invite students to illustrate the poster with drawings of their dads; then display it in your classroom.

Dads Are...

fun

good singers

good basketball players

silly

helpful

good at cooking outside

big

workers

Dads In Print And In Person

Share one or more of these stories about dads. Better yet, invite some fathers to come in as guest readers!

My Dad Is Awesome
Written by Nick Butterworth
Published by Candlewick Press

Can I Help?
Written by Marilyn Janovitz
Published by North-South Books

Octopus Hug
Written by Laurence Pringle
Published by Boyds Mills Press

Guess How Much I Love You
Written by Sam McBratney
Published by Candlewick Press

A Ditty About Dad

This clap-and-slap chant will have youngsters rhyming in rhythm as they tell about all the wonderful things dads do! Teach the words to the chant; then show youngsters how to alternately clap their hands and slap their hands on the floor as they chant each word. Have them slap the floor three times in succession at the end of each line. This cheer will get your little ones fired up about fathers!

(chanted to the rhythm of "A Sailor Went To Sea, Sea, Sea")

Dad helps me brush my teeth, teeth, teeth.
He likes to read me books, books, books.
He helps me tie my shoes, shoes, shoes.
Sometimes he even cooks, cooks, cooks.

Dad really likes to play, play, play.
His stories are first-rate, -rate, -rate.
He always makes me laugh, laugh, laugh.
My dad is really great, great, great!

Daddy Dress-Ups

Little ones love dressing up like Dad—especially when they have a special box full of grown-up clothing! Duplicate the note on page 59 and send a copy home with each child. While you're waiting for the donations to arrive, have youngsters help you decorate a big cardboard box to hold all the daddy gear. Hunt through parenting magazines and tear out pictures of dads and children together. Invite your students to use paintbrushes and diluted glue to attach the pictures to the box. Once the glue is dry, the box is ready to hold ties, vests, baseball caps, pajamas, hiking boots, and more. What a wonderful permanent addition to your dramatic-play area!

Daddies On Display

This interactive bulletin board puts fathers in the spotlight. To prepare, ask each child to draw a portrait of her father. (Provide face outlines to help younger students get started.) Mount all the pictures on a bulletin board titled "Guess Who!" Below each portrait, mount an envelope with the flap facing outward. Into each envelope slip a piece of paper with the dad's identity printed on it. Invite students and visitors to guess whose father is pictured in each drawing, then check their guesses by peeking into the envelopes.

Stripes And More Stripes

Send Father's Day greetings in classic stripes with this printmaking project. In advance, make a tagboard tracer of the necktie pattern on page 59. For each child, trace the pattern onto a folded sheet of construction paper, so that the top of the tie is on the fold. (You'll be able to trace three ties onto a folded sheet of 12" x 18" paper.) Cut out the ties through both layers to create greeting cards that open from bottom to top.

To have youngsters create stripes on the ties, try one of these methods (or use one for the front and one for the back of each card):

— Cut a 5" x 10" strip of corrugated cardboard. Peel away the top paper layer to expose the ridges. Brush tempera paint over the ridged strip; then press the tie-shaped card onto the painted cardboard to make a print.
— Glue 1/2-inch-wide strips of felt along the length of a cardboard paper towel tube. Roll the tube through a shallow tray of tempera paint; then roll the tube over the necktie card, from bottom to top.

Once the paint has dried, invite each child to write, copy, or dictate a Father's Day message on the inside of her card. Have her sign her name before presenting the card to her dad.

Gift Ideas For Dad

Gifts made by little hands are always special! Try one of these this Father's Day.

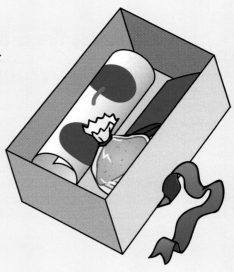

Have A Berry Nice Day, Dad!

Here's a tasty gift that will start Father's Day on a yummy note. First, have your little ones help you prepare a few batches of blueberry muffins, using your favorite prepackaged mix. Make the muffins extra special by adding some fresh blueberries to the batter. Pour the batter into muffin tins lined with paper muffin cups. While the muffins are baking, have each child decorate a placemat for Dad to use at his special breakfast. Give each child a sheet of 9" x 12" white construction paper with the message "Happy Father's Day!" printed on it. Provide bingo markers full of blue ink or blue tempera paint. Have each child make blue dots around the message on his paper. Have him add tiny blueberry stems with a green marker. Laminate the finished placemats for durability.

Help each child assemble her gift. Have her place a plastic-wrapped muffin into a shoebox, along with her rolled-up placemat and a blue napkin. Help her tie the shoebox with a blue ribbon. Dads will surely enjoy these "berry" special treats!

Worth The "Weight"

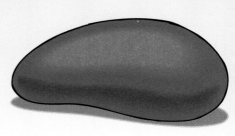

For a more lasting gift, have your youngsters make these colorful paperweights for their dads. In advance, bury a class supply of small rocks (plus a few extra) in your sand table. Provide shovels and ask students to visit the table in small groups. Have each child dig up the perfect rock for her dad. Once everyone has a rock, have each child color her rock with crayons. Place the colored rocks on a foil-lined baking sheet. Pencil each child's name on the foil near her rock. Bake the rocks for 15 minutes at 250°. After the rocks cool, have each child glue a small piece of felt to one flat side of her rock to create a paperweight. Help each child wrap her gift in pretty tissue paper and ribbon before sending it home.

Make It A Party!

If your school or center is open around Father's Day, invite dads to school for a special event in their honor. Have youngsters dress up like their dads (see "Daddy Dress-Ups" on page 57) and perform the chant in "A Ditty About Dad" (page 56). Invite dads to find their portraits (see "Daddies On Display" on page 57). Serve muffins on child-decorated placemats (see "Have A Berry Nice Day, Dad!") and invite youngsters to present their fathers with cards (see "Stripes And More Stripes" on page 57) and gifts (see "Worth The 'Weight'"). No doubt about it—dads will be delighted!

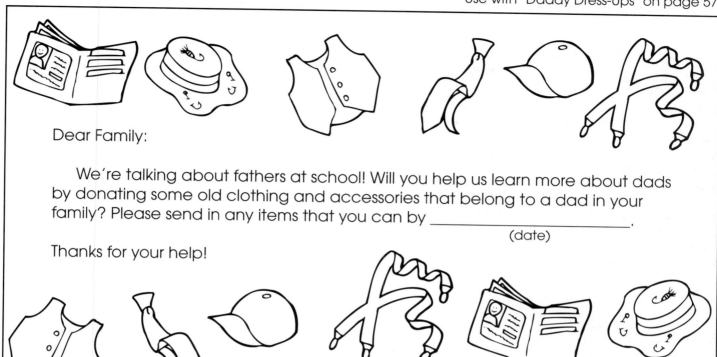

Dear Family:

We're talking about fathers at school! Will you help us learn more about dads by donating some old clothing and accessories that belong to a dad in your family? Please send in any items that you can by _____.
(date)

Thanks for your help!

Necktie Pattern
Use with "Stripes And More Stripes" on page 57.

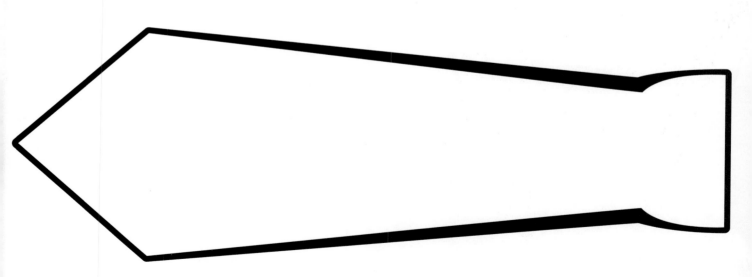

Oh! Say, Can You See...

Light up some Fourth of July fun with this sparkling Independence Day unit that focuses on the symbols of the holiday! These red-hot ideas are sure to have your little patriots seeing stars!

ideas contributed by Michele Dare and Nancy Lotzer

Declarations Of Independence

For many youngsters, Independence Day means hot dogs, barbecues, and fireworks at night. Help them learn the true meaning of the holiday by discussing how colonial America declared independence from British rule. Explain that the colonists wanted to rule themselves or be *independent*. If possible, show a copy of the Declaration of Independence to your class. Next have each student name something that she can do independently, and then illustrate it on an enlarged copy of the pattern on page 63. Help her complete the sentence at the bottom of the pattern; then have her sign her name. Display students' completed work on a bulletin board titled "Our Declarations Of Independence," or bind the pages into a class book with the same title.

History In The Singing

Your youngsters' knowledge of history will skyrocket when you teach them this informative Fourth of July jingle. Be sure to define and discuss with your students the more difficult words in the lyrics such as *liberty*. Before long, your little ones will really be "in tune" with the meaning of Independence Day!

Independence Day
(sung to the tune of "Clementine")

Back in 1776, our Founding Fathers did declare,
"We're independent, independent
From the British over there!"

So they fought for, so they fought for,
So they fought for liberty!
To be a country independent,
Independent, proud, and free.

Now, on the Fourth of, on the Fourth of,
On the Fourth, Fourth of July,
We celebrate our nation's birthday
With fireworks up in the sky!

I Pledge Allegiance

Use this all-American activity to help your youngsters learn some flag facts while sharpening their visual-discrimination skills. Write each line of the rhyme below on a sentence strip; then laminate the strips. Place the strips in a pocket chart near your classroom's U.S. flag. Then create cards with words, numbers, or pictures that match those in the rhyme, and then place them in a container near the pocket chart. Invite a small group of children to help you examine the flag and recite the rhyme. Have a student pull a card from the container, and match it to the word or number in the pocket chart. When all the cards have been matched, recite the rhyme together one last time. Your little patriots are sure to be flag-smart after this activity!

Stars And Stripes For Me And You!

50 stars for 50 states,
On a field of blue,
With 13 stripes of red and white
Made for me and you!

50 ☆ for 50 states,
On a field of blue,
With 13 stripes of red and white
Made for me and you!

Flag Match

This center idea will have little hearts beating true for the red, white, and blue! Duplicate two enlarged copies of the flag pattern on page 63. Color both copies, laminate them, and then cut them out. Place one flag on a cookie sheet or other magnetic surface. From the second flag, cut out the individual stripes and the blue field of stars. Place a strip of magnetic tape on the back of each piece. Challenge your little ones to match the cut-out stars and stripes with the stars and stripes on the second flag. As they work, encourage them to recite the rhyme from "I Pledge Allegiance."

And The Rocket's Red Glare...

Your little ones will have a blast with this supervised outdoor rocket experiment! Obtain a class supply of Fuji® film canisters with lids. Around each canister, use a permanent marker to draw a line 1/4 inch from the bottom. Then have each student use red, white, and blue paint markers to decorate his canister (rocket). Create a rocket launcher by using duct tape to secure a toilet-paper tube to a plastic plate. Make several extra launchers to replace those that become worn during the activity.

To send the rockets into space, you will need a package of Alka-Seltzer® tablets, a container of water, and the rocket launchers. Outside, prop a launcher at an angle, aiming it toward a vacant area away from people. Have each child dip his rocket into the container and fill it to the line with water. Hold the rocket as he drops 1/4 of an Alka-Seltzer tablet into it. Immediately replace the cap tightly and then place the rocket, cap-side down, into the launcher. Stand back and start counting the number of seconds until blast-off (approximately 15). Record each rocket's launch time; then graph the results if desired. After discussing the graph, have children hypothesize how the tablets launched the rockets. Now there's an experiment that will send your class into orbit!

Here's how it works: When mixed with water, Alka-Seltzer tablets produce gas bubbles. The pressure from the bubbles forces the canister to separate from its top, launching the canister into the air!

Liberty Bell Pudding Pops

Use this easy snack idea to introduce your little ones to another Independence Day symbol—the Liberty Bell! To make an edible bell, fill a plastic wine glass with butterscotch pudding. Place a piece of a chocolate graham cracker in the pudding as shown, making sure that the edge of the cracker is visible through the side of the glass. Insert a craft stick in the middle of the pudding and then place the glass in the freezer. When the pop is half-frozen, place a gumdrop clapper in the pudding. Keep the pops in the freezer overnight. Then set the glasses in warm water and gently pull out the pops. Have your youngsters sing the song below before biting into these bells of freedom. What a way to ring in some snacktime fun!

The Liberty Bell Song
(sung to the tune of "Row, Row, Row Your Boat")

Ring, ring, ring the bell!
Ring for Liberty!
Ding-a-ling, ding-a-ling,
Ding-a-ling, ding-a-ling!
Crack! It broke! Dear me!

Liberty Bell Facts

- The Liberty Bell was originally called the Old State House Bell because it had been ordered for the State House in Philadelphia. It did not become known as the Liberty Bell until 1839.
- It cracked on its first ringing and had to be recast.
- It was rung on July 8, 1776, to announce the adoption of the Declaration of Independence.
- The Liberty Bell weighs over 2,080 pounds and was purchased for around $300.

Stars And Strips Forever!

Your youngsters will shine brightly with these patriotic headbands that reinforce patterning skills. Have each student glue a pattern of red, white, and blue stars onto a sentence-strip headband. Staple the headband to fit the child's head; then help her staple thin strips of laminating film to the inside of the headband. Next have her glue a star to the end of each strip of film, and then decorate the stars with markers or glitter-glue pens. Have students wear their star-spangled headgear as they march around the room to some patriotic music. For added Fourth of July fun, tie red, white, and blue streamers to each child's arms. Hooray for the red, white, and blue!

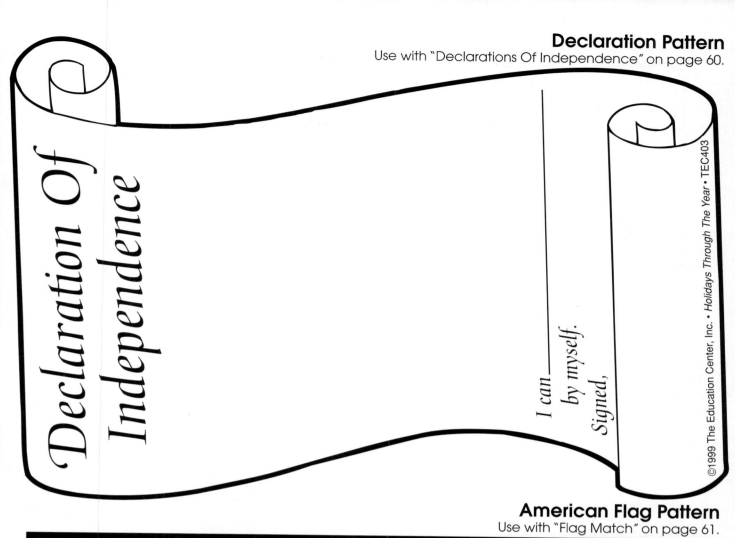

Declaration Of Independence

I can ___ by myself.
Signed, ___

©1999 The Education Center, Inc. • *Holidays Through The Year* • TEC403

American Flag Pattern
Use with "Flag Match" on page 61.

Grandparents Are Great!

National Grandparents Day is the Sunday after Labor Day. Use the ideas in this unit to celebrate the importance of grandparents in the lives of many young children. If you have students who do not have living grandparents (or have little contact with their grandparents), suggest that they focus on older adult friends for these activities. Soon your youngsters will agree—grandparents are grrrrreat!

ideas contributed by Lori Kent and Betty Silkunas

Nice To Meet You

Put together this photo album to showcase the grandparents and older friends of your class. Prior to the start of your unit, use the note on page 67 to request photos of grandparents or other older adult friends from each family. As the photos arrive at school, make a copy of each one and label the copy with the corresponding child's name; then return the original photo. (Provide photos of some older school volunteers or other familiar adults for any child who does not bring a photo.)

To make a grandparents' album, invite each child to glue her photocopied picture to a sheet of colorful construction paper. Then encourage her to use markers, stickers, and die-cuts to decorate her album page. Invite her to write or dictate some of the experiences she has shared with this grandparent or older friend. Place the pages in a purchased photo album or bind them together between laminated construction-paper covers. Share the album during a group time, inviting each child to tell about her page. Then add the album to your book area for students to enjoy during free-choice time.

I love Grandma Midgie. She reads to me.

Oh, I Love My Grandparents

Students will soon be singing the praises of their grandparents when you teach them this sweet song. Invite students to think of other appropriate verbs to substitute for the underlined words.

(sung to the tune of "The More We Get Together")

Oh, I love my grandma,
My grandma, my grandma.
Oh, I love my grandma,
And she loves me.
We [sing] and we play.
We [giggle] all day!
Oh, I love my grandma,
And she loves me.

Oh, I love my grandpa,
My grandpa, my grandpa.
Oh, I love my grandpa,
And he loves me.
We [talk] and we play.
We [read books] all day!
Oh, I love my grandpa,
And he loves me.

My Grandparents Live			
in the same house as I do	in the same city as I do	in the same state as I do	in a different state
Sarah Robin	A.J. Cassi Adrienne Sam	Carly Ben Jacob Peter Hannah	Jessie Molly Seth David

Where In The World Is Grandpa?

Some grandparents live in the same house as their grandchildren; others live half a world away! Explore distances with this fun activity. Begin by requesting envelopes addressed to grandparents (see the request note on page 67). Once the envelopes arrive, prepare a chart (similar to the one shown) with appropriate categories for the addresses of your children's grandparents or older adult friends. Invite each child to write his name under the appropriate category (or categories). Then compare. Whose grandparents live the closest? Whose live the farthest away? How many grandparents live in the same city? The same state? Further illustrate the range of distances by posting a state or national map on a bulletin board. Use pushpins to mark your location and the cities and towns in which the children's grandparents reside. Then use the envelopes you collected for the following activity.

Love Notes

Whether they live near or far, grandparents love pictures of their grandchildren! Give little ones an opportunity to send a photo and a note to their grandparents or older adult friends. If you haven't already done so, use the note on page 67 to request envelopes addressed to each child's grandparents or older adult friends. Throughout one day at school, snap a photo of each child doing something he particularly enjoys. Have the photos developed; then have multiple copies made for those children who have brought in more than one envelope.

With envelopes and photos ready, give each child a small construction-paper heart for each of his envelopes. Write his dictated message to his grandparent(s) on one side of a heart; then invite him to decorate the opposite side with markers or glitter pens. Then have him tuck a photo and a heart-shaped note into each of his envelopes before sealing it. Mail these heartfelt notes off to some happy grandmas and grandpas!

Joshua in the math learning center.

I love you Nana!

Dressing Up

Your little ones are sure to enjoy dressing up like grandparents in your dramatic-play area. If possible, request that students' grandparents send in some dress-up items, such as sweaters, purses, scarves, hats, and jewelry. Store all the items in a big box or trunk. Be sure to snap some photos of your dressed-up youngsters. My, oh my—you look good for your age!

"When I Was Young..."

Invite your students to send some unique Grandparents Day greetings. In advance, request or purchase a supply of inexpensive audio cassette tapes. You'll need one tape for each grandparent or set of grandparents in each child's family. Explain to your little ones that whether their grandparents are 40 or 80, a lot has changed since they were little! Then invite them to make a tape for each of their grandparents (or sets of grandparents) telling about their lives today and asking about their grandparents' lives when they were young.

Help each child, in turn, place a cassette tape in your tape recorder. Have her first record a Grandparents Day greeting, then record some information about herself and her current interests, such as her favorite food, movie, toy, book, or clothing. At the end of her taping, have her ask her grandparent(s) to record similar information about when he or she was young. Label each tape with the recipient's name; then send the tapes home, along with a copy of the note on page 67. Families will treasure this bit of recorded history!

Where Are Grandma's Glasses?

Review the pictures in your grandparents' photo album (see "Nice To Meet You" on page 64). Talk about the fact that many older people wear glasses. Teach youngsters the traditional fingerplay "Grandma's Glasses." Then invite them to make glasses cases as thoughtful Grandparents Day gifts. (Even grandparents with perfect vision probably wear sunglasses!)

Prepare by cutting a flannel-backed vinyl tablecloth into 4" x 19" pieces. Fold each piece in half; then use a hole puncher to punch holes one inch apart along the two long sides. To make a case, a child laces a 12-inch length of yarn through the holes on one side, knotting the yarn at the top and bottom holes as shown. Then she repeats the lacing and knotting on the other side. If desired, provide dimensional paints for decorating the cases. What an eye-catching gift!

Here are Grandma's glasses.	*Use fingers to form circles around eyes.*
Here is Grandma's hat.	*Use hands to form cone shape over head.*
And this is the way she folds her hands	*Fold hands.*
And puts them in her lap.	*Rest hands in lap.*
Here are Grandpa's glasses.	*Use fingers to form circles around eyes.*
Here is Grandpa's hat.	*Use hands to form cone shape over head.*
And this is the way he folds his arms.	*Fold arms across chest.*
Just like that!	*Nod head.*

Parent Request Note

Use with "Nice To Meet You" on page 64 and "Where In The World Is Grandpa?"
and "Love Notes" on page 65.

Dear Family:

We are talking about grandparents at school. Could you help us with our activities by providing the items checked below?

_____ a photo of each of your child's grandparents or sets of grandparents (or an older adult friend)
(Please label each photo with your child's name. These will be returned as soon as we make photocopies to use in an activity.)

_____ a stamped, addressed envelope for each of your child's grandparents or sets of grandparents (or an older adult friend)

Please send these items to school by _____.
                                                    (date)

Thank you for helping to make our unit more meaningful to your child!

©1999 The Education Center, Inc. • *Holidays Through The Year* • TEC403

Dear Family:

As part of our learning about grandparents, we've recorded a special Grandparents Day greeting on this cassette tape. Please give it or send it to the designated grandparent(s) or adult friend(s). On it, your child has recorded information about his or her interests. It includes a request for your child's grandparent(s) or adult friend(s) to record something about his or her life as a young child and then to return the tape to your child as a keepsake. I hope your entire family enjoys this intergenerational sharing!

©1999 The Education Center, Inc. • *Holidays Through The Year* • TEC403

Happy Birthday, Johnny Appleseed!

September 26 marks the birth of John Chapman, also known as Johnny Appleseed. Celebrate the life of this famous American with these apple-oriented activities. They'll please your apple lovers to the core!

ideas contributed by Suzanne Moore

Thank You, Johnny!

Pique your youngsters' curiosity about Johnny Appleseed by sharing the interesting facts below or by reading *Johnny Appleseed* by Patricia Demuth (Grosset & Dunlap). After reading the story, revisit the page that shows the different apple dishes prepared by the settlers. Then serve up some cold cider. As the children enjoy this cool, refreshing drink, brainstorm other ways apples can be prepared to eat. Jot down all student suggestions.

Duplicate a class supply of the booklet page on page 71; then have each of your little apple lovers illustrate her favorite apple dish. Have each youngster write her name and label her dish in the provided spaces. Share the illustrations during circle time. Then bind the pages into a class book titled "Thank You, Johnny Appleseed!" Mmmm…delicious reading!

Thank You,
Johnny Appleseed!
by
Ms. Robert's
Class

Katie
(Name) loves apple muffins , yes, indeed!
Thank you, Johnny Appleseed!

Appleseed Facts

- Johnny Appleseed (1774–1845) knew about apples because he grew up in New England. His real name was John Chapman.
- Johnny traveled through the Midwest, planting apple seeds along the way.
- He got his apple seeds from cider mills.
- At least once a year, he returned to check on the seeds he planted.
- Johnny was a friend to settlers and Native Americans, selling and giving away apple trees to all.

Apple "Sense-ation"

Celebrating Johnny Appleseed's birthday is also the perfect springboard for studying another topic ripe for learning—the five senses! Read the parent note and poem on page 71 with your class. Have each child decorate and personalize a copy of the note and then glue it onto a small lunch bag; then send home the bag. On celebration day, invite small groups of children to fully examine their washed apples. As they investigate, encourage your youngsters to describe what they see, feel, smell, hear, and taste. Prepare an apple-shaped chart for each small group and record their descriptions on it. After all students have investigated their apples, use the charts during circle time to compare each group's findings. Display the completed charts. Invite your apple explorers to find matching words and practice reading the descriptive vocabulary on the charts.

Apple-Oriented Centers

On Johnny Appleseed's birthday, provide lots of hands-on experiences for your little ones with the following learning centers:

Sand Table: Stock this center with a variety of small gardening tools and apple seeds to give your budding gardeners plenty of practice planting seeds.

Math Area: Place a variety of apples in this area. Invite students to sort the apples, sequence them from smallest to largest, and create different patterns with them. If desired, include a balance and measuring tape and encourage your youngsters to weigh and measure the apples.

Play-Dough Area: Spur students' pie-making imaginations by stocking this center with plastic apples, foil pie pans, rolling pins, and cinnamon-scented play dough.

Reading Area: Gather up a bushel of books about apples and Johnny Appleseed. Decorate your reading corner with a large construction-paper apple tree; then add the projects from "Stuffed Apples" (right) to the tree.

Dramatic Play: Set up a fruit stand with plastic apples and other fruits nestled in baskets. Provide an apron, paper bags, and plenty of play money for customers!

Stuffed Apples

Making these artistic apples will be bushels of fun for little hands! Spread red fingerpaint on a cookie sheet. Have a student make patterns in the fingerpaint; then lay a large piece of art paper on top of her completed painting. Help her smooth the paper with the palm of her hand; then slowly peel off the paper. When the paint is dry, cut out two large same-sized apple shapes from the fingerpainted paper. Help each youngster staple the lower two-thirds of both apple shapes together back-to-back. Gently stuff the shape with a crumpled, plastic grocery bag; then staple around the remainder of the apple. Next have each child use a permanent marker to write her name on green felt leaves. Glue or staple the leaves to the top of the apple. Finally, create a mouthwatering display by hanging these spectacular 3-D apples on the tree in your reading center (see "Apple-Oriented Centers").

Appetizing Applesauce

Set up an apple center for those children who would like to help chop apples for applesauce. In advance, cut several apples into fourths. Lightly coat the pieces with lemon juice to prevent browning; then place them in a bowl. After demonstrating safe slicing procedures, invite each child to wash her hands thoroughly and then visit the center to chop apples with plastic knives. Have students place the apple bits in a separate bowl; then use these pieces in the applesauce recipe below. Serve this special treat during Johnny's birthday celebration (see "Celebrate With Applesauce!" below). Your little folks will love this homemade dish, and the apples will make your room smell heavenly!

Applesauce
(makes 3 cups)

8 apples, peeled, cored, and chopped
1/2 cup water
1/2 teaspoon ground cinnamon
1/2 cup packed brown sugar
1 tablespoon butter

Place all ingredients except butter in a large pot. Cover and cook on medium heat until the apples are tender (about 40 minutes). Mash the apples with a potato masher and stir in the butter before serving.

Celebrate With Applesauce!

Wrap up Johnny's birthday celebration by singing "Happy Birthday To You" and then serving some Appetizing Applesauce to your little ones. Afterward, sing this song to thank Johnny for planting all those seeds and growing all those apples.

(sung to the tune of "London Bridge")

Johnny planted apple seeds,
Apple seeds, apple seeds.
Johnny planted apple seeds.
Thank you, Johnny!

The apple seeds grew into trees,
Into trees, into trees.
The apple seeds grew into trees.
Thank you, Johnny!

The trees grew apples on their limbs,
On their limbs, on their limbs.
The trees grew apples on their limbs.
Thank you, Johnny!

We pick the apples in the fall,
In the fall, in the fall.
We pick the apples in the fall.
Thank you, Johnny!

Thank you, Johnny Appleseed,
Appleseed, Appleseed.
Thank you, Johnny Appleseed.
Thank you, Johnny!

_____ loves _____, yes, indeed!
(Name)

Thank you, Johnny Appleseed!

Apples, apples, picked from the tree,
This fruit is really good for me.
Thank Johnny Appleseed for this snack.
And bring an apple in this sack!

Dear Parents,

Did you know that September 26 is Johnny Appleseed's birthday? Our class plans to celebrate by learning about apples. Please send **one apple of any color** in this sack on _____ (date).

Thanks!

Celebrate Columbus Day

Ahoy, matey! Sail with your seafaring students into this cross-curricular unit commemorating Columbus's journey to the New World.

by Mackie Rhodes

Set Sail With Columbus

Sail into your Columbus Day studies with this activity. To begin, share the facts below with your class; then mark both Spain and the Indies on a globe using separate pieces of Sticky-Tac. Using additional pieces of Sticky-Tac, attach a length of yarn to show the common route from Spain to the Indies during Columbus's time. Then attach another yarn length to show Columbus's intended route across the Atlantic to the Indies. As students observe, lead them to discover that the new route did not lead Columbus directly to the Indies—some unknown islands and land masses blocked his way. Although Columbus believed he had reached the Indies, he had actually reached a New World! Tell youngsters that Columbus had arrived in the land known today as the Americas.

- Columbus was an explorer who wanted to find a shorter route to the Indies.
- Columbus hoped to find gold in the Indies.
- In Columbus's time, many believed that one had to sail around Africa to get to the Indies—a region including India, China, the East Indies, and Japan.
- Columbus believed he could reach the Indies by sailing west.
- On August 3, 1492, Columbus set sail from Spain with three ships—the *Niña*, the *Pinta*, and the *Santa María*.
- Land was first sighted from the *Pinta* on October 12, 1492. A cannon was fired to mark the occasion.
- Columbus had discovered a New World unknown to Europeans. Today this land is known as the Americas.

It's Home To Me

Teach youngsters this song about Columbus's historic voyage to America, our homeland.

(sung to the tune of "Twinkle, Twinkle, Little Star")

In fourteen hundred and ninety-two,
Columbus sailed the ocean blue.
From miles of sea to solid ground,
A brand-new world his crew had found.
Columbus and his ships of three
Found the land that's home to me!

Point thumb towards back.
Sail flat palm across front of body.

Hold hand over brow.
Hold up three fingers.
Point to self.

Ships Of Three

Enlist your crew's help in replicating Columbus's three ships; then have students fill these ships with phonetic cargo. To make a ship, attach an upright yardstick to one end of a medium-sized box. Tape a poster-board sail to the yardstick. Write the name of one of Columbus's ships—*Niña, Pinta,* or *Santa María*—on each of the three box ships. Then point out the beginning letter sound of each ship's name. (*Santa María* has two initial letter sounds, of course!) Invite each child, in turn, to find an item with an initial sound corresponding to one of the ships. Have her place the item in the ship. (For large items, place a notecard labeled with the item's name in the ship.) Then review each ship's cargo of phonetic finds. Afterward have students unload the ships and reload them with new batches of cargo.

Niña, Pinta, Santa María!

Reinforce the names of Columbus's ships with this game similar to Duck, Duck, Goose. Have students sit in a circle on the floor. Appoint a child to be Columbus. To play, ask Columbus to walk around the seated students. As he passes behind each child, instruct him to tap the child on the head while naming one of the ships. When Columbus names *Santa María*, the tapped child gets up and chases Columbus around the circle. Then repeat the game, assigning the role of Columbus to the chaser. Continue play as long as student interest dictates.

In The Crow's Nest

Outfit youngsters to discover some interesting sightings of their own with this idea. For each child, duplicate the hat pattern (page 75) on brown construction paper. Have each child cut out her pattern, then glue her cutout onto a construction-paper headband. Fit her headband to her head; then staple the ends together.

Tell students that sailors on ships like those of Columbus often climbed up to the crow's nest of a ship to observe and give a report of their surroundings. Most likely land was first sighted from this vantage point on the *Pinta*. Invite each child, in turn, to climb into an imaginary crow's nest to observe her surroundings through a paper towel–tube telescope. Have her describe one of her sightings in I Spy fashion while her shipmates try to guess the item. Invite the mate who correctly guesses the described item to make the next climb into the crow's nest.

Seafaring Messages

Youngsters will have a barrel of fun at your water table when they role-play Columbus. Before setting up this activity, tell students that Columbus encountered many dangers during his return voyage. He feared that he might not safely return to Spain, so he wrote about his findings. He sealed his writings in a cask—a barrel-shaped container—and threw the cask overboard in the hopes that someone would find his message.

Gather a few empty, plastic, barrel-shaped containers from powdered soft drink mixes. Remove the labels and place the empty containers at your water table. Set paper and crayons on a table nearby. Invite each youngster at this center to draw or write a message. Have him fold or roll his paper, place it in a container, and then screw the cover on tightly. Have him sail his message-in-a-barrel across the water-table sea for a fellow sailor to read or interpret.

A New World Of New Flavors

Along with the New World, Columbus was introduced to many new foods. Bring in some of these foods (see the list below) and show them to your youngsters. Ask them to pretend they've never seen these foods before. (They may *not* have seen some of them!) What names would they give them? Would they try cooking or eating them? Can they think of other uses for them? After checking for allergies, offer some of these foods as a Columbus Day snack.

New World Flavors

corn	avocados	peanuts
potatoes	papayas	cashews
tomatoes	peppers	pecans
beans	pineapples	chocolate
pumpkins	blueberries	

Searching For Gold

Here's a golden opportunity to encourage your young explorers to practice their counting skills. In advance, spray-paint a large supply of pebbles with gold paint to represent gold nuggets. Hide the nuggets in an outdoor area. Remind your class that Columbus hoped to find gold in the Indies; then invite students to set out on a gold hunt. Instruct each child to place her gold nuggets into her own paper bag. Afterward, ask her to count and report her findings to the class. Then group several students together and have them count their combined nuggets. Finally, have the class chorally count all of the gold nuggets. Congratulations! Your class just struck it rich in counting.

HALLOWEEN HAUNTINGS

Boo! It's Halloween time again, and you know what that means—costumes, candy, pumpkins, and carnivals. Turn your classroom into a frighteningly fun carnival guaranteed to make every ghoul grin!

ideas contributed by Connie Walker

Shapely Masks

What better way to get your little carnival-goers ready than with these geometric masks? To prepare, cut out a supply of construction-paper shapes in various colors and sizes. Also cut a pair of 1½-inch eyeholes in a class supply of paper plates. Glue or tape a tongue depressor handle to the front of each plate. Put the plates in a center with the paper shapes, glue, and markers or crayons.

To make a shapely mask, have a child think of an animal or another mask design possibility. Ask her to select several paper shapes, identify them, and then glue the shapes onto the back of the plate to create her mask. When the glue is dry, have her add features with markers or crayons. After each child has made a mask, have a classroom masquerade march! For added learning fun, ask each child to compare and contrast the shapes on the masks.

Mary Wore A Clown Mask

After making the masks described on this page, put them to use with this musical activity. Gather students into a circle. Discuss how a person looks different when he wears a mask, even though he is still the same underneath. To demonstrate this concept, invite each child, in turn, to hold his mask in front of his face as the rest of the class looks on. Then sing this song with students, featuring each child's name and mask in a different verse. When a child hears his name, have him hold his mask in front of his face. See, it's just little ol' me—and my mask!

(sung to the tune of "Mary Wore Her Red Dress")
[Mary] wore her [clown] mask,
[Clown] mask, [clown] mask.
[Mary] wore her [clown] mask
For Halloween!

Designs On You

Your little ones will delight in this face-painting station. Use the recipe below to make several different colors of face paint. (Or purchase inexpensive commercial face paint in costume stores.) Enlarge onto construction paper several simple designs from which students may choose, such as pumpkins, clown features, animal noses, hearts, and stars. Be sure to check with parents about possible skin allergies before beginning this activity. Also recruit a few adult volunteers to help at this station.

During the carnival, invite each child, in turn, to choose one design. Thinly apply the paint with small paintbrushes. Caution each wearer to allow the paint to dry. There you have it—perfectly painted faces to accompany your crew's carnival costumes!

clown

animal

Face Paint
2 parts cornstarch
1 part original formula cold cream (not "ultra" formula)
1 part water

Mix the ingredients together; then divide the paint into small lidded containers. To each container, add a different food coloring, drop by drop, until the paint is the desired color. Tightly cover the paint until ready to use. This paint keeps well.

Punkin Chunkin'

This gross-motor center is sure to be a hit with your little tricksters! In advance, cover three large, clean, empty cans with orange construction paper (or spray-paint them orange). Use a black marker to draw a jack-o'-lantern face on each can. Decorate a supply of orange beanbags to resemble pumpkins. Set the pumpkin cans on the floor in an open area. Place a strip of masking tape on the floor a desired distance from the cans to indicate where a child should stand to use this center. Also place a basket of treats (such as stickers) nearby.

To play, a child stands on the masking-tape line and gently tosses a pumpkin beanbag into one of the cans. Encourage the child to toss the remaining beanbags into the cans in a like manner. Then invite her to choose a treat from the basket.

Spooky Sensory Stew

Mmm—gooey pumpkin stew! Serve up a batch of this truly yucky (and inedible!) stew in your sensory area and have your young scientists dig right in. To prepare, carefully carve a medium or large pumpkin with students, scooping the seeds, pulp, and flesh into a clean sensory tub or plastic cauldron. If desired, add chunks of pumpkin left over from carving jack-o'-lantern features. Invite pairs of youngsters to see, smell, and stir the stew with their bare hands. This stew won't last long, so make sure everyone has a turn in the same day. After everyone has investigated the pumpkin stew, discuss its appearance, scent, and texture. For more language fun, invite students to dictate recipes for the stew and describe the creatures that might eat it!

Monster Match

Remember the old-fashioned cakewalk game? This small-group variation will boost visual discrimination while little ones happily stomp to the beat! In advance, duplicate onto construction paper two sets of the cards on page 79. Color and laminate the cards; then cut them apart. Tape one set of cards to the floor in a large circle. Place the other set in a trick-or-treat bag or a plastic pumpkin.

Invite each of six children to find a card on which to stand. To play one round, play some lively music and have the group march around the circle. Stop the music and have each child stand on the nearest card. Announce "Monster Match!", draw a card from the container, and show it to your youngsters. Help the group find the matching card; then invite the child standing on the match to become the matching monster and draw the next card. Return the card to the container and turn the music on to resume play. Continue rounds of play until each child has had a turn to be the matching monster. For added fun, change the type of movement when you change monsters. Try asking the group to crawl, skip, hop, jump, tiptoe, or monster stomp around the circle. They'll do the match—the monster match!

Jack-O'-Science

When the carnival ends, you're faced with slightly used jack-o'-lanterns and pumpkins. Don't toss them—use them for scientific observation! Put a carved pumpkin (or a piece of a pumpkin) in a shallow pan. Place another pumpkin (or piece) in a clear, airtight container, and seal the container. Set the two containers in the classroom where students can easily observe them. Finally, place a third pumpkin (or piece) outdoors in a secluded spot. On each of several days, invite each child to use a magnifying glass to observe the three pumpkins (or pieces). If desired, ask each child to draw a picture of what he sees. Encourage children to compare the three. The pumpkin in the sealed container will provide weeks of scent-free, interesting observation. Hey, it's not gross—it's science!

Tales For Your Tricksters

Choose from these books as well as your old favorites for a thrilling mix of sweet and spooky stories!

Six Creepy Sheep
Written by Judith Ross Enderle and Stephanie Gordon Tessler
Published by Boyds Mills Press, Inc.

Apples And Pumpkins
Written by Anne F. Rockwell
Published by Aladdin Paperbacks

The Little Old Lady Who Was Not Afraid Of Anything
Written by Linda Williams
Published by HarperTrophy

Pumpkin Pumpkin
Written by Jeanne Titherington
Published by Mulberry Books

We're Goin' On A Wild Turkey Chase!

Oh, no! Thanksgiving is just around the corner, and the prized bird has suddenly taken flight! Lead your youngsters on a wild turkey chase with these ideas and activities that will have your flock gobbling with delight!

by Michele Dare

Turkey On The Loose!

Help! Help! Thanksgiving dinner just flew the coop! Get your youngsters ready to go on a wild turkey chase with this fine-feathered fingerplay.

Gobble, gobble, gobble!
What's all the fuss?
Clever Mr. Turkey is hiding from us!
Let's look all around.
Don't let him get away!
We need that turkey on Thanksgiving Day!

Flap elbows up and down like wings.
Hands up, questioning.
Hands cover eyes.
Hand to brow, look around.
Shake index finger.
Pat stomach.

Wanted: One Big Fat Turkey

Don't let that turkey get away! Have your youngsters make Wanted posters for the bird at large. In advance, program a sheet of paper similar to the Wanted poster shown; then duplicate it for each child. Examine with your students different pictures of turkeys and discuss what turkeys look like. Give each child a Wanted poster and direct her to draw a picture of the runaway bird. Next have her write a reward amount beside the dollar sign. Encourage the child to dictate some words that describe the turkey; then write her response on her poster. Mount these Wanted signs throughout the school and let that turkey know that you mean business!

Track 'em Down!

In order to find the runaway bird, your little ones will need some basic turkey training. Help them recognize the tracks of a turkey with this activity. Duplicate a copy of the bird and track patterns on page 83. Color the patterns, laminate them, and then cut them out. Glue a strip of felt to the back of each cutout. During circle time, help your youngsters identify each bird cutout. Then place the birds and tracks on a flannelboard. Invite student volunteers to match each bird with its track. When students are familiar with this activity, place the patterns at your flannelboard center for children to use independently. Watch out, Mr. Turkey! We're hot on your trail!

Turkey Footprints

Tracking down that turkey will be easy with this potato-print art activity. Cut several large potatoes in half. Use a permanent marker to draw a turkey track (as shown) on the flat side of each half. Then cut away about a half inch of the surrounding potato as shown. Place the potatoes and several shallow pans of paint at your art center. Invite students to dip the potato printers into the paint, then make turkey-track prints on a sheet of construction paper. When the paint is dry, help each youngster cut around his tracks and write his name on the back of each one. After the children have left for the day, tape the tracks on the walls and ceiling of your room. If desired, place a few colorful feathers around the room. When your little ones return the following morning, watch as their eyes grow wide with excitement. That turkey's been in our room, and look at the mess he's made!

Setting A Turkey Trap

What is a turkey's favorite snack? Berries! Set up this "berry" clever math center to try to lure Mr. Turkey out of hiding! Label ten plastic or paper bowls, each with a different number from 1–10. Explain to students that turkeys love to eat berries; then place a bowl of dried cranberries at the center. Direct students to set out a snack for Mr. Turkey by placing the appropriate number of cranberries in each bowl. As an extension, challenge students to sequence the numbered bowls before placing the cranberries in them. Here turkey, turkey, turkey!

Turkey Treats

Is that bird still at large? Don't despair! You can still serve up a tasty holiday turkey without him! Have your little ones follow the recipe shown to make a Thanksgiving treat that everyone will love, including Mr. Turkey himself!

Turkey-In-The-Straw

Ingredients for one snack:
$1/2$ cup of vanilla pudding
crumbled shredded wheat cereal
1 small round sugar cookie
1 Tbsp. of white frosting
yellow frosting in a tube
6 pieces of candy corn
2 M&M's Minis® candies
1 red hot

Half-fill a clear, wide-mouth cup with vanilla pudding. Then add crumbled, shredded wheat cereal over the top of the pudding. Next spread white frosting on a small, round sugar cookie. For feathers, add six pieces of candy corn in the frosting near the top of the cookie. Squeeze a tube of yellow frosting to make a triangle beak in the center of the cookie as shown. Then place M&M's Minis® candies in the yellow frosting for the eyes. Add one red hot below the tip of the triangle for the turkey's wattle. Place the cookie in the shredded wheat and pudding; then eat!

Some Juicy Turkey Tales

A Turkey For Thanksgiving
Written by Eve Bunting
Published by Clarion Books

Gracias The Thanksgiving Turkey
Written by Joy Cowley
Published by Scholastic Trade

'twas The Night Before Thanksgiving
Written by Dav Pilkey
Published by Orchard Books

Thanksgiving At The Tappletons'
Written by Eileen Spinelli
Published by HarperCollins Juvenile Books

Track Patterns
Use with "Track 'em Down!" on page 81.

Duck

Chick

Turkey

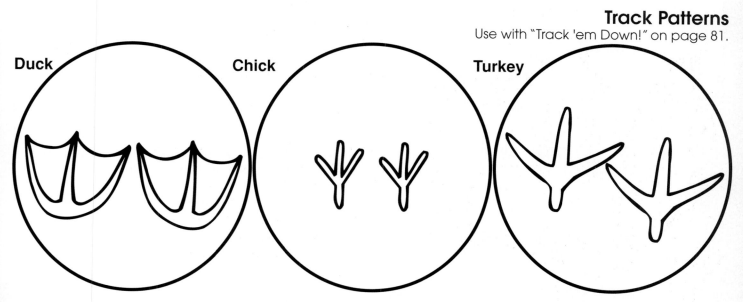

Happy Hanukkah!

If you are on the hunt for fresh Hanukkah ideas, look no further! This unit is filled with fun and exciting activities to help introduce your youngsters to this ancient Jewish holiday.

ideas contributed by Barbara Spilman Lawson and Michele Dare

Hanukkah Begins Tonight

Begin your Hanukkah study by discussing some of the holiday's symbols and traditions. Duplicate the picture cards on page 87; then color the cards and laminate them for durability. As you discuss the various Hanukkah symbols and traditions, show your youngsters the corresponding cards. When students are familiar with these items, teach them the poem below. Distribute the picture cards to five student volunteers. As each line of the poem is recited have a child hold up the appropriate picture card.

Hanukkah Begins Tonight

Little candles burning bright.
Hanukkah begins tonight.

Dreidels spinning, what a sight.
Hanukkah begins tonight.

Chocolate gelt, I'll take a bite.
Hanukkah begins tonight.

Latke pancakes fried just right.
Hanukkah begins tonight.

Many presents wrapped up tight.
Hanukkah begins tonight.

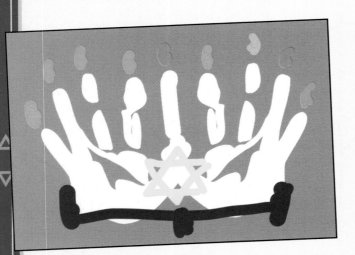

Handmade Menorahs

Your youngsters will be eager to get their hands on this art activity. Prepare a shallow tray of white tempera paint mixed with a little dish detergent. Working with one or two children at a time, invite each student to press one hand at a time into the paint and then onto a sheet of blue construction paper as shown. When the handprints are dry, have each student paint a tall *shammash* candle that extends up from her thumbprints. Then direct her to paint orange flames above each fingerprint so her handprints resemble a lit menorah. Finally, allow each child to decorate her menorah using blue and yellow paint.

- The shammash, *the tallest candle on the menorah, is used to light the other candles.*
- *Blue, white, and yellow are traditional Hanukkah colors. Blue and white are the colors in the Israeli flag. Yellow symbolizes the glow of Hanukkah candles.*

Delicious Latkes

In remembrance of the miraculous oil, many Jewish families serve *latkes* (potato pancakes fried in oil). Give your youngsters a taste of this traditional Hanukkah dish by following the recipe below.

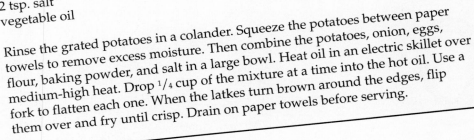

Potato Latkes

(makes approximately 20 latkes)

12 medium potatoes, peeled and grated
2 small onions, grated
4 eggs, beaten
4 Tbsp. all-purpose flour
$1/2$ tsp. baking powder
2 tsp. salt
vegetable oil

Rinse the grated potatoes in a colander. Squeeze the potatoes between paper towels to remove excess moisture. Then combine the potatoes, onion, eggs, flour, baking powder, and salt in a large bowl. Heat oil in an electric skillet over medium-high heat. Drop $1/4$ cup of the mixture at a time into the hot oil. Use a fork to flatten each one. When the latkes turn brown around the edges, flip them over and fry until crisp. Drain on paper towels before serving.

Latke Flip

After making potato latkes, set up this fun center to help your youngsters practice their eye-hand coordination. Stock the area with several small frying pans and pretend latkes, such as plastic canister lids, beanbags, or circles cut from heavy cardboard. Challenge students to place a pretend latke in the frying pan, gently flip it in the air, and then catch it in the pan. Encourage students to count how many times they can flip the latke without dropping it. Or invite pairs of students to use the pans to flip the latke back and forth. Now there's an activity your youngsters will flip over!

Spin, Dreidel, Spin!

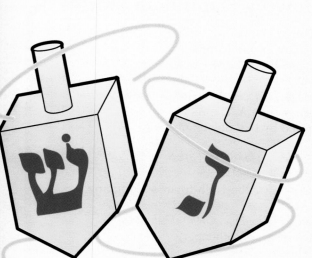

The *dreidel*, a spinning top used in a Hanukkah game, is another well-known symbol of the holiday. Obtain a dreidel for your youngsters to examine; then use this circle-time activity to help reinforce visual discrimination skills. In advance, duplicate the picture cards on page 87 several times so there are enough cards for each child to have one. Then duplicate a set of pictures for yourself. (Or use the set previously made for "Hanukkah Begins Tonight" on page 84.) For durability, laminate the cards before cutting them apart. Give each child one picture card. Next hold up a picture from your set and invite those children with matching cards to stand up, spin like a dreidel, and then sit back down. Continue playing until all children have had a chance to spin.

Gelt Patterns

While *gelt* is the Yiddish word for money, it also refers to chocolate coins wrapped in gold foil. During Hanukkah, many children receive gelt, both real and chocolate. Use this golden center idea to help reinforce your youngsters' early math skills. On yellow construction paper, duplicate the coins on page 87 several times. Laminate the coins; then cut them out. Place the coins in a pouch and invite students to sort the coins or make patterns with them. When youngsters have sorted successfully or have completed a pattern, reward them with a piece of gold-foil-wrapped chocolate gelt.

Pass The Present

During Hanukkah's eight-day celebration, many gifts are exchanged among loved ones. Use this fun adaptation of Hot Potato to help reinforce your little ones' manners and teach them the joy of giving. Wrap a small box with holiday wrapping paper and ribbon. Have the children sit in a circle and pass the present as you play a lively musical selection. When the music stops, direct the child holding the present to turn and thank the student who handed it to him. Then have the gift giver respond accordingly. After the exchange, start the music again and resume passing the present. Happy Hanukkah, everyone!

Glowing Hanukkah Stories

The Chanukkah Guest
Written by Eric A. Kimmel
Published by Holiday House, Inc.

The Magic Dreidels: A Hanukkah Story
Written by Eric A. Kimmel
Published by Holiday House, Inc.

The Borrowed Hanukkah Latkes
Written by Linda Glaser
Published by Albert Whitman & Company

Inside-Out Grandma: A Hanukkah Story
Written by Joan Rothenberg
Published by Disney Press

Hanukkah Picture Cards
Use with "Hanukkah Begins Tonight" on page 84,
and "Spin, Dreidel, Spin" on page 85.

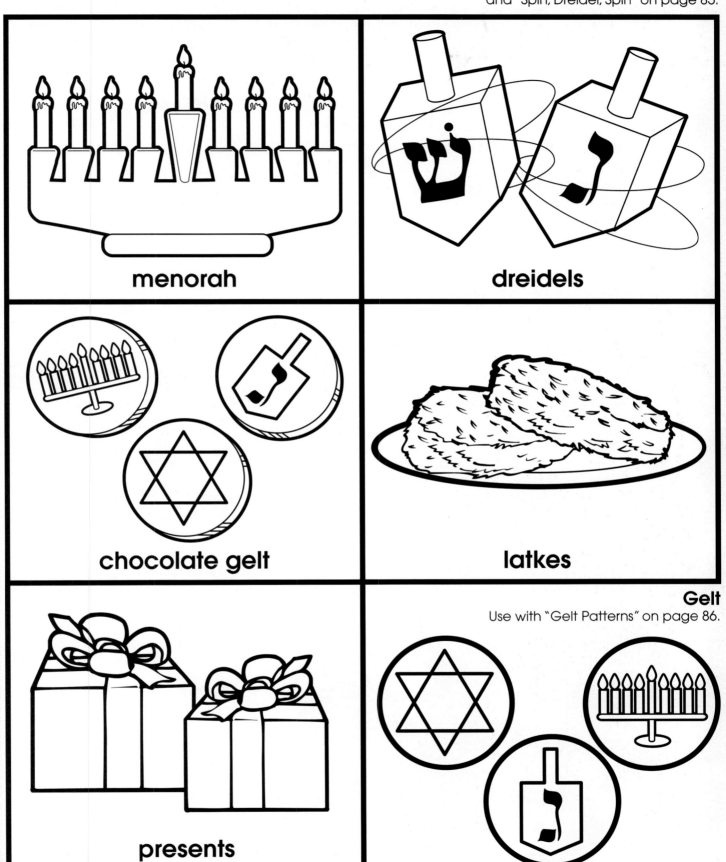

menorah

dreidels

chocolate gelt

latkes

presents

Gelt
Use with "Gelt Patterns" on page 86.

ELF-TRAINING PROGRAM

A spokesperson for Santa Claus claims that due to an increase in good boys and girls this year, Santa needs extra helpers. The advertisement on the right appeared in the *Polar News and Tribune*. Are your children qualified for the positions? Use the ideas in this elf-training program to get them ready to apply!

ideas contributed by Elizabeth Fritz

HELP WANTED
Elves needed to craft and wrap gifts, assist in care and feeding of reindeer, and perform other elfish tasks to be designated by S. Claus. Excellent benefits. Apply at North Pole.

ELF ATTIRE

Every good elf needs a uniform, so be sure your little elves are dressed for success by helping them make caps to wear on the job. For every four children, cut a felt circle that is 36 inches in diameter. Then cut the circle into quarters as shown. To make one cap, overlap the straight edges of one of the pie-shaped quarters so that it forms a cone that fits a child's head. Use embroidery floss and a large needle to sew the cone closed. (Older children may complete this step with assistance.) Also sew several jingle bells to the tip of the cap. Use dimensional fabric paint to label each child's cap; then, when the paint is dry, invite him to use additional dimensional paint to decorate his cap. When each child's cap is complete, have him dress for work by donning his cap and putting on an apron. Reporting for duty!

FA, LA, LA, LA

Hardworking elves make the time fly by singing while they work. Teach your job candidates this song, and then have them march together as they sing.

SANTA'S ELVES

(sung to the tune of "Jingle Bells")

Santa's elves, Santa's elves
Work hard every day
Building toys and wrapping gifts,
Then sending them your way. Hey!

Santa's elves, Santa's elves
Have a lot to do
Working hard to make the toys
That Santa brings to you! Yea!

REINDEER CRUNCHIES

Sure, Santa likes a little treat during his long Christmas Eve ride, and so do his reindeer! Have your elves make these simple treats for those fantastic flying friends. To prepare the treat, a child spreads peanut butter on at least two large pretzel sticks. Next she places mini chocolate chips on the peanut butter. After eating one treat herself, she wraps the remainder in colorful plastic wrap, tying the package closed with curling ribbon.

by Elf Toby

COMMUNITY SERVICE

Community service is an integral part of an elf's duties. Have your elves make these placemats to share with folks at an elder care facility or homeless shelter. Ask each child to use crayons or other art supplies to decorate a 9" x 12" piece of construction paper. Laminate the placemats; then deliver them along with a class note wishing the recipients happy holidays from all your little elves.

BUSY MAKING GIFTS

Elves check Santa's lists to see who has been naughty and who has been nice; then they get busy making gifts. Help each of your children think of a family member or adult friend who has been nice to him. Then help him make a lantern that person will appreciate! To make one lantern, the child paints the outside of a baby food jar with water-diluted glue. Next he places squares of two different colors of tissue paper over the jar, smoothing and overlapping the squares as he covers it. While the glue is wet, he sprinkles on glitter so that the lantern glimmers when it is lit. Finally he puts a votive candle inside. Now the lantern is ready to be wrapped!

WRAPPING 101

Presentation of gifts is the final part of an elf's duties. To practice, have your little ones decorate tissue paper to wrap up their lanterns (see "Busy Making Gifts" on page 89) or other presents. Invite each child to repeatedly dip the ends of cardboard tubes into tempera paint and then onto sheets of tissue paper. Allow the paper to dry. Next set up a gift-wrapping station with tape, scissors, markers, and curling ribbon. In addition, duplicate a number of gift tags (page 91) to include in the area. Invite a child to bring his decorated sheets and a gift to the area. After wrapping his present, have him color and cut out a tag to attach to it.

REQUIRED READING FOR ELVES

Elf Help: http://www.falala.com
Written by Margie Palatini
Published by Hyperion Books for Children

The Oldest Elf
Written by James Stevenson
Published by Mulberry Books

The Last Christmas Present
Written by Matt Novak
Published by Orchard Books

ELF CERTIFICATION

Congratulate your elf trainees with a certification ceremony. In advance, duplicate a class supply of the certificate on page 91. Color each certificate, if desired, and personalize it. In pencil, write each child's initials on one corner of the back of her certificate; then roll it so the initials are visible from the outside. Tie a length of curling ribbon in a bow around the rolled certificate. During the ceremony, give a speech similar to the following:

Congratulations to all of our honorary elves! You have demonstrated hard work, good listening skills, artistic talent, and cooperation with your fellow elves. I hereby present each of you with a certificate of completion of the elf-training program.

After giving each child her certificate, complete the program by singing some Christmas songs, including "Santa's Elves" (page 88). You might also want to prepare a treat of cookies and punch for the new elves. Who knows? Maybe Santa himself will show up at the reception!

This is to certify that on this day—December_____, _____—

_____

(child's name)

has successfully completed

S. CLAUS & CO.'S OFFICIAL ELF- TRAINING PROGRAM

CELEBRATE KWANZAA!

From December 26 to January 1, Kwanzaa is celebrated by African-American families to honor their African heritage. Highlight this holiday with these ideas to help youngsters understand the symbols and customs of Kwanzaa.

ideas contributed by Vicki Mockaitis Dabrowka

SEVEN PRINCIPLES, SEVEN SYMBOLS

Here are the pronunciations and meanings of the Swahili words expressing the principles and symbols of Kwanzaa. Use these and information gathered from the books recommended below to help you share information about this holiday with your students.

Principles:
1) *Umoja* (oo-MOH-jah): unity
2) *Kujichagulia* (koo-jee-chah-GOO-lee-ah): self-determination
3) *Ujima* (oo-JEE-mah): collective work and responsibility
4) *Ujamaa* (oo-jah-MAH-ah): cooperative economics
5) *Nia* (NEE-ah): purpose
6) *Kuumba* (koo-OOM-bah): creativity
7) *Imani* (ee-MAH-nee): faith

Symbols:
* *Kikombe cha umoja* (kee-KOHM-bee chah oo-MOH-jah): a unity cup used to toast one's ancestors
* *Kinara* (kee-NAH-rah): a candleholder which holds seven candles
* *Mazao* (mah-ZAH-oh): crops (fruits and vegetables) which represent the importance of planting, harvesting, and working together
* *Mishumaa saba* (mee-shoo-MAH-ah SAH-bah): the seven candles representing Kwanzaa (three red, three green, and one black)
* *Mkeka* (em-KEH-kah): a woven mat symbolizing tradition and history
* *Vibunzi* (vee-BOON-zee): ears of corn which represent the children in one's family
* *Zawadi* (zah-WAH-dee): gifts to symbolize the commitment between parents and children

BOOKS ABOUT KWANZAA

For the teacher:

Kwanzaa: A Family Affair
Written by Mildred Pitts Walter
Published by Lothrop, Lee & Shepard Books

It's Kwanzaa Time!
Written by Linda and Clay Goss
Published by G. P. Putnam's Sons
(Includes stories, activities, songs, and recipes for Kwanzaa.)

For students:

A Kwanzaa Celebration Pop-Up Book
Written by Nancy Williams
Published by Little Simon Books

Seven Days Of Kwanzaa: A Holiday Step Book
Written by Ella Grier
Published by Viking Children's Books